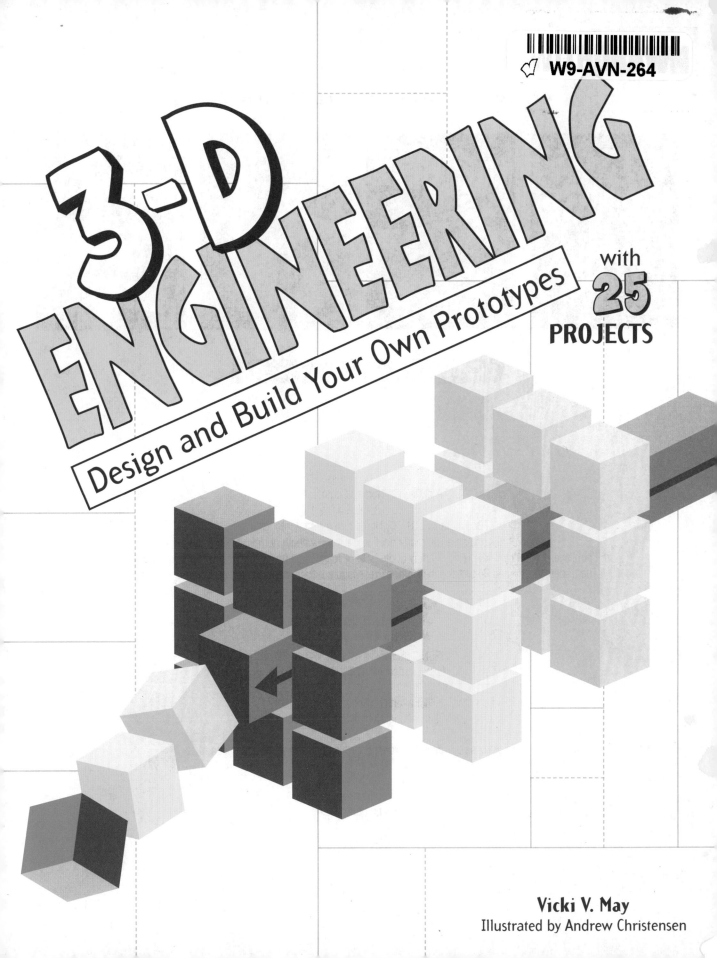

3-D ENGINEERING

with **25 PROJECTS**

Design and Build Your Own Prototypes

Vicki V. May

Illustrated by Andrew Christensen

~ Latest science titles in the *Build It Yourself* Series ~

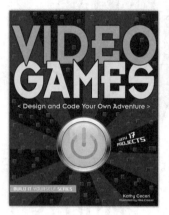

Check out more titles at www.nomadpress.net

Nomad Press
A division of Nomad Communications
10 9 8 7 6 5 4 3 2 1

This book was manufactured by Marquis Book Printing,
Montmagny, Québec, Canada
November 2015, Job #115324

ISBN Softcover: 978-1-61930-315-7
ISBN Hardcover: 978-1-61930-311-9

Illustrations by Andrew Christensen
Educational Consultant, Marla Conn

Questions regarding the ordering of this book should be addressed to
Nomad Press
2456 Christian St.
White River Junction, VT 05001
www.nomadpress.net

Printed in Canada.

CONTENTS

PS

INTERESTED IN PRIMARY SOURCES?

Look for this icon. Use a smartphone or tablet app to scan the QR code and explore more about engineering! You can find a list of URLs on the Resources page.

If the QR code doesn't work, try searching the Internet with the Keyword Prompts to find other helpful sources.

3-D engineering 🔍

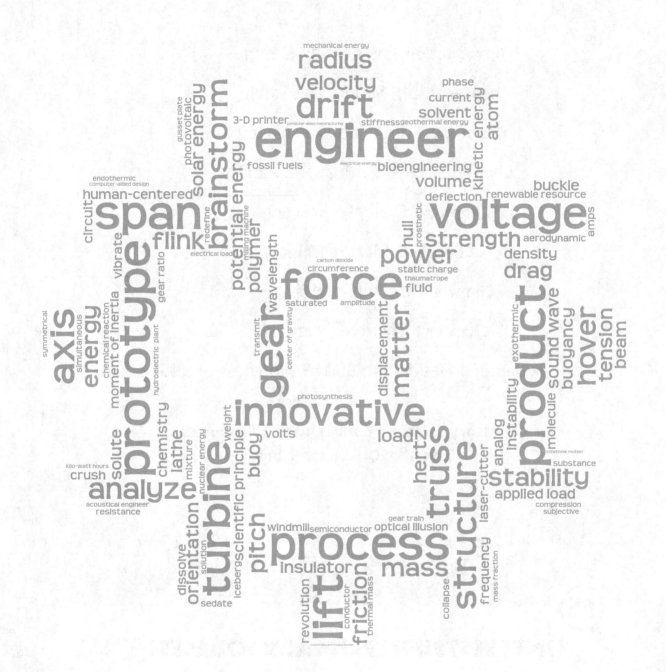

ENGINEERING DESIGN

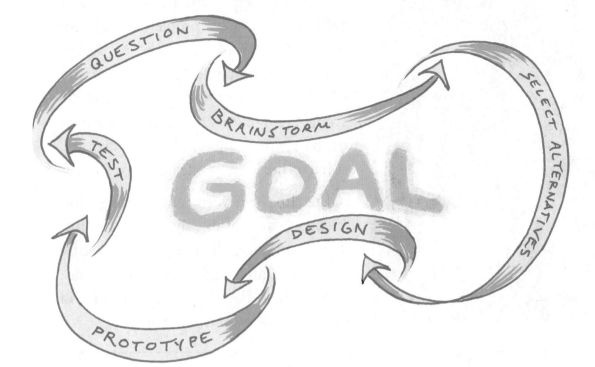

What are some of the things you use every day? How were they made? How do they work? How did the ink get inside your pen? How do the gears shift on your bike? How do we get the electricity you use for lights and television?

Engineers design products used by people all over the world. These products include cars, toys, buildings, movie animation, computers, iPhones, water filters, medical procedures and devices, and wind turbines. Just about everything that's built was designed by an engineer!

WORDS 2 KNOW

gear: a rotating part with teeth.

engineer: someone who uses science, math, and creativity to design products or processes to meet human needs or solve problems.

turbine: a machine with blades turned by the force of water, air, or steam.

1

Engineers apply math, science, and **technology** to solve problems and meet goals. What would you like to design and build? Guidelines for designing and building a tower of raw spaghetti strands strong enough to hold a marshmallow can be found at the end of the chapter. What other design ideas do you have?

The line between engineering and science can often be blurry. But scientists tend to discover new **scientific principles** and engineers apply science and math so they can design and build new **products** and **processes**.

For example, Isaac Newton discovered the laws of motion and Henry Ford applied those laws to design automobiles. A Swiss mathematician named Daniel Bernoulli discovered the principle of lift in the 1700s and the Wright brothers used this principle to design an airplane.

> "Scientists investigate that which already is; engineers create that which has never been."
> —**Albert Einstein**

Scottish scientist James Clerk Maxwell discovered electricity and magnetism, which Thomas Edison applied when he designed the light bulb.

DID YOU KNOW?

Post-it notes were the result of a failed experiment. Dr. Spencer Silver, a scientist at 3M, set out to create a super-strong adhesive. One of his "failed" **prototypes** turned out to be the pressure-sensitive adhesive now used in Post-it notes.

What does it mean to design? The design process involves a few different steps.

ENGINEERING DESIGN PROCESS

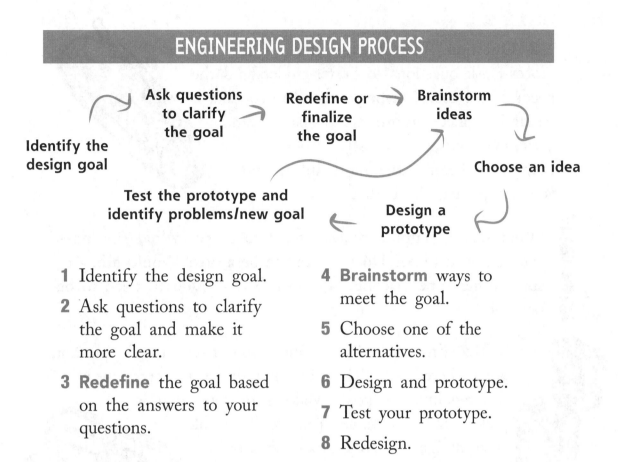

Identify the design goal → Ask questions to clarify the goal → Redefine or finalize the goal → Brainstorm ideas → Choose an idea → Design a prototype → Test the prototype and identify problems/new goal

1 Identify the design goal.

2 Ask questions to clarify the goal and make it more clear.

3 **Redefine** the goal based on the answers to your questions.

4 **Brainstorm** ways to meet the goal.

5 Choose one of the alternatives.

6 Design and prototype.

7 Test your prototype.

8 Redesign.

While you probably don't realize it, you are designing something when you draw a picture, build with Legos, and even when you put together your outfit for the day.

Let's look closely at all the steps of the design process. You'll find examples of these steps in the red type.

1 Identify the Goal. The first step is to identify your design goal. Are you trying to solve a problem, improve a product or process, or meet a need?

Let's design a box to carry school supplies. Throughout the design process, you'll refine your design goal.

3

2 Question. During this step of the design process, ask questions to better understand the needs of the user. Maybe you need to conduct research, collect information, observe and interview users, or investigate what has been done before. The more information you can gather, the better.

What school supplies do you need to carry? What size does the box need to be? Does it need to be a box? Would a bag or some other type of container work better? Does it need to be portable?

3 Redefine the Goal. Once you have asked questions and gathered additional information, you might need to redefine the goal. Make sure your goal is clear and achievable. You won't be able to design an appropriate solution if you don't understand the goal. This redefined goal is clearer and includes information from the questioning phase.

Design a way to store and easily transport four to six pencils, a pencil sharpener, and a large eraser. The case does not need to be lockable, but does need to be easy to carry and easy to open. The length of a typical pencil is 7½ inches. Be sure to measure your supplies before building your case!

> "Design is not just what it looks and feels like. Design is how it works."
>
> **—Steve Jobs, founder of Apple**

4 Brainstorm. During the brainstorming phase, come up with LOTS of ideas, including crazy ones, and write them down. You may choose to brainstorm alone or in a group. If you brainstorm with a group, be sure to be positive about all ideas, encourage craziness, and don't judge.

- A custom-sized wooden or cardboard box
- A pouch into which the pencils and supplies may be rolled and tied
- A piece of pipe or bamboo or other tube with one end blocked and a removable covering on the other end
- Skip the pouch or box altogether and simply tie or Velcro the supplies into your backpack

DID YOU KNOW?

Engineers design and build roller coasters and other rides in amusement parks. The Millennium Force roller coaster is more than 300 feet high with cars that travel more than 90 miles per hour on the roller coaster.

FABULOUS FABRIC

Fabric may not seem like a traditional engineering material, but many engineering systems use fabric-like material. Fabric has been used as sails on sailboats, roofs of buildings, water filters, and biomedical devices. The roof of the Denver International Airport is built of a fabric-type material.

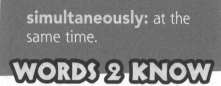

5 Select Alternatives. Remember your design goal? Do all of your ideas meet that goal? You might have to carefully evaluate the pros and cons of different ideas to decide which ones to try. Always record your reasons for selecting different alternatives in your design journal.

Select a pencil case design made out of a piece of bamboo with a piece of fabric over the top because it sounds like a pretty unique solution and meets your design goal. Also select a fabric pouch, because it will be a lightweight and a flexible solution.

6 Design and Build a Prototype. Sketch out different design ideas and build a prototype. Building prototypes is a critical part of the design process. It's a good idea to build lots of models as early in the process as possible. These models don't need to be fancy—they can be made out of paper and tape or other easy-to-find materials.

Designing and prototyping should happen **simultaneously**. The best designs occur after a lot of prototyping. Rather than spend hours and hours making your design drawings perfect, jump in and build a prototype!

For your first pencil box prototypes, use paper to experiment with shapes and designs, switching to scraps of fabric as you refine your design. Experiment with fabric coverings for a bamboo case, pouches with pencils rolled inside, pouches with flaps, and pouches with zippers. Instead of using a real zipper in the initial prototypes, try tape.

6

7 **Test Your Prototype:** Keep in mind that most prototypes will not work perfectly—many will fail to work at all. Don't get discouraged! Engineers learn just as much, if not more, from failed prototypes as they do from the ones that work. Once a prototype works, you can try to make it better.

Which shape made the best pencil box? Which material was the most useful? Remember your design goals. Is your pencil box easy to carry and open? Do your pencils, pencil sharpener, and eraser all fit?

8 **Redesign Your Prototype:** Once you have a prototype that seems to meet your needs, think of ways to redesign it to make it even better.

Try using some fun fabric that fits your style. How about adding a button or other decoration to the front?

DID YOU KNOW?

Through the engineering design process, engineers came up with the idea to add dimples to golf balls to help them fly better.

Engineers are continually improving the products you use regularly, such as bicycles, smartphones, and refrigerators. They also work on ways to help people and the environment, including designing artificial limbs and medicines and finding ways to clean up oil spills.

This book will guide you through the engineering design process so that you can build many different prototypes. Each chapter will explore a key engineering principle through designing and prototyping.

Remember, this is only a guide—you can modify the designs as you wish to meet your needs and design goals.

We'll use math, science, and technology along with the design process to meet human needs and find different engineering solutions. Building prototypes will help you learn. Many prototypes will fail to work at first—that's okay! Failure is just one step on the path to success. Without failure, we wouldn't learn very much.

> "Successful engineering is all about understanding how things break or fail."
>
> **—Henry Petroski, engineer specializing in failure analysis**

GOOD ENGINEERING PRACTICES

Every good engineer keeps a design journal! Choose a notebook to use as your design journal. As you read through this book and do the activities, keep track of your ideas, design processes, results, and ways in which you can improve your prototypes.

Each chapter of this book begins with an essential question to help guide your exploration of engineering.

? **ESSENTIAL QUESTION**

What is engineering and how does it impact your life?

Keep the question in your mind as you read the chapter. At the end of each chapter, use your design journal to record your thoughts and answers.

MARSHMALLOW CHALLENGE

SUPPLIES
20 strands uncooked spaghetti ♦ 1 yard tape
1 yard string ♦ 1 marshmallow ♦ timer

Try the Marshmallow Challenge, a fun and quick design challenge that thousands of people have attempted.

1 Design Goal: In 18 minutes, build the tallest freestanding **structure** that can support a marshmallow. Check out the official rules on the website before you get started to answer any questions.

marshmallow challenge 🔍

2 Brainstorm: Alone or in a group, think of ideas for creating your structure. Because of the time limit, keep your brainstorming to a couple minutes.

3 Select Alternatives: Decide on which design to do, plus a few other designs to try. Make sure your ideas meet the goals. Will it hold the marshmallow? Is it tall?

4 Design and Prototype: Draw a quick sketch, then start to build. Try several different designs.

5 Test and Reflect: When the time is up, measure the height of your tower. What worked? What didn't work? What could be improved?

WORDS 2 KNOW

structure: something that is built, such as a building, bridge, tunnel, tower, or dam.

Kids usually have the tallest structures because they start building prototypes quickly and learn what does and doesn't work. Adults spend too long planning on paper!

SAFETY FIRST!

Building prototypes involves cutting foamcore and cardboard and gluing with a glue gun. Using these tools safely is important.

Tips for Cutting Foamcore and Cardboard

❑ Use an X-Acto knife with lots of blades, not a mat knife.

❑ Use a metal ruler that has cork or masking tape on the backside to prevent slipping. The wider the ruler, the easier it is to hold.

❑ Use the back of a pad of newsprint as a cutting surface.

❑ With your hand on the far edge of the ruler, hold the ruler over the part you want to keep and guide the blade along the other edge. This keeps your hand as far from the blade as possible and keeps the ruler from slipping.

❑ Use the whole blade to cut, not just the tip.

❑ Use three strikes to make one cut. First, score the surface paper. Second, cut the surface paper and some foam. Third, cut the remaining foam and bottom paper.

❑ Blades go dull very quickly, and cuts from dull blades heal more slowly than cuts from sharp blades.

❑ Never kneel on the board—you might cut your knee!

❑ Always wear shoes—sometimes, blades fall off tables.

❑ Think! Where will the blade go if it slips? Be aware!

Tips for Using a Glue Gun

❑ Be careful! The tip gets hot!

❑ A glue gun is a great tool for building prototypes since the glue dries quickly and sticks to most surfaces. You can purchase a hot glue gun at a hardware store, craft store, or any place that sells office and school supplies.

❑ To be safe, use a low-temperature glue gun and only with an adult's supervision. You can also get glue guns with automatic shut-offs.

❑ Place your glue gun on a piece of paper to protect your work surface.

Chapter 1

STIFF, STRONG, AND STABLE

When you drive over a bridge, what keeps that bridge from collapsing? After all, there might be hundreds of cars on the bridge at one time—that's a lot of weight. Why doesn't the bridge simply fall down? What makes a tower, building, set of crutches, step ladder, or anything solid that supports a load stay standing?

WORDS 2 KNOW

collapse: to fall in or down suddenly.

weight: a measure of the force of gravity on an object.

load: the weight of something.

? **ESSENTIAL QUESTION**

How does an engineer design a structure to support a load?

stiffness: the ability of an object to resist deflecting or moving when a load is applied.

strength: the ability of an object to support a load before breaking.

stability: the ability of an object to maintain a certain position without collapsing.

beam: a structural element that resists bending under the weight of a load.

orientation: the position of a beam relative to the applied load.

Many people might say that a structure must be "strong" to support a heavy load. But it is actually a combination of **stiffness**, **strength**, and **stability** that keeps a structure upright and allows it to support a load.

What can you design and build that is stiff, strong, and stable? You'll find guidelines to the following projects at the end of the chapter. Use your imagination to design and build other things, too!

- A stability structure that is beautiful and stable, but looks unstable.

- A chair made of only cardboard and duct tape.

- A bridge that will bear a load.

STIFFNESS

Have you ever heard of something being described as stiff? It means that the object doesn't bend or deflect easily.

Some materials are stiffer than others. What factors do you think affect stiffness? Will a wood **beam** be as stiff as a steel beam? How about two beams of different lengths? Does the way the beam is held up matter? How about beams with different shapes or with different **orientations**?

Using a ruler, you can find the answers to these questions by experimenting. Bend the ruler and then bend a piece of paper of the same size. Do both materials bend the same? Which one is easier to bend?

Hold the ruler at one end and push down on the other end. Then hold it at the middle and push down on the end. Which is stiffer, or deflects the least, the longer ruler or the shorter ruler? Does length have an effect on stiffness?

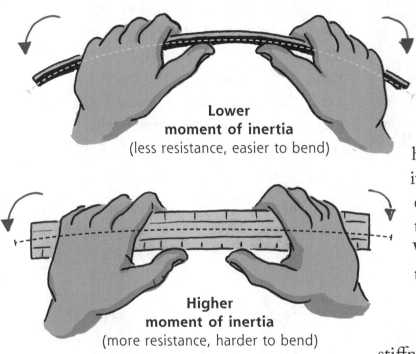

**Lower
moment of inertia**
(less resistance, easier to bend)

**Higher
moment of inertia**
(more resistance, harder to bend)

Bend the ruler while holding it flat and bend it while holding it on its edge. This is a test of the ruler's orientation. Which way is it easier to bend?

Material, length, and orientation all affect stiffness. So does the shape. Stiffer materials such as steel will be harder to bend than wood or cardboard. Shorter beams are also stiffer.

It's easy to see that the ruler bends more easily when you hold it flat, but why? The answer has to do with something called the **moment of inertia** and whether it is high or low.

Imagine a line drawn through the middle of the ruler. This line is called the central **axis**. The moment of inertia measures an object's **resistance** to bending around that central axis.

WORDS 2 KNOW

moment of inertia: the measure of an object's resistance to bending. It is a geometrical property that relates to the distribution of mass in a shape.

axis: the center, around which something rotates.

resistance: a **force** that slows down another force.

force: a push or a pull.

13

The farther the **mass** of the ruler is away from the central axis of the shape, the higher the moment of inertia and the stiffer the ruler will be. The closer the mass of the ruler is to the central axis, the lower the moment of inertia, and the more easily the ruler bends.

Which of these shapes has the lowest moment of inertia? Which has the highest? Which shape bends the easiest?

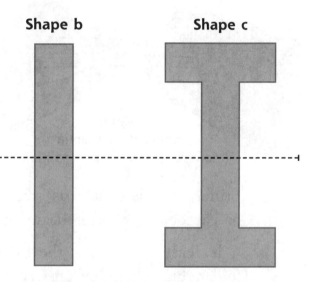

Shape b

Shape c

Shape a

The flat rectangle (a) has the lowest moment of inertia and is the least stiff because all of its mass is close to the central axis represented by the dotted line. The I-beam (c) is the stiffest and has the highest moment of inertia because it has the most mass farther away from the central axis. Which shape might you use to build a bridge?

STRENGTH

Strength is the ability of something to support loads before breaking. Strength depends on the type of material used to support the load. It also depends on the type of load being applied and whether it is a pulling or pushing load or a bending load. Rope, for example, is strong when it is pulled but cannot be pushed or bent.

compression: a pushing force that squeezes or presses a material inward.

crush: to break apart.

buckle: to collapse in the middle.

WORDS 2 KNOW

Experiment with several different materials, including rope, wood, chalk, and licorice. First, try pulling on each material. Can you break any of the materials? Now try bending the materials. What happens? Did any of them break?

What happens if you push on each of the materials? This is called **compression**. Two things can happen when you push on a material. It will break apart, called **crush.** It will crumple in the middle and **buckle.** When a material buckles, it cannot support any additional load.

STABILITY

Stability is the ability of an object to keep a certain position or shape without collapsing. What happened to the piece of rope when you pushed on it? The rope probably started collapsing in the middle, which is called buckling. Buckling is a stability issue.

instability: not stable.

center of gravity: the point on any object where all the weight is centered.

WORDS 2 KNOW

When you push on a long, slender object too hard, it has a tendency to shift outward at the middle and eventually collapse. This is called a buckling failure and is one example of **instability**.

Stability is also important in structures. When you pile books in a stack, you have to pay attention to the **center of gravity** of the books. Otherwise the stack of books will come tumbling down.

Stack books up one on top of the other, with each extending out from the first as shown here. How tall can you stack the books? How far can you extend each level?

If the books extend too far over, the stack will collapse. But how far is too far? And why will it collapse?

For each book, the center of gravity, or the point through which the weight acts, is at the center of the book. If you stack a book so its center of gravity rests on the book below it, the book will remain in position. If you stack a book so its center of gravity does not rest on another book below it, the book is likely to fall over. That's a stability failure!

16

Towers are affected by stability, too. When the center of gravity falls within the base of the tower, the tower is likely to remain stable and upright. Once it leans over far enough so the center of gravity falls beyond the base, the tower will probably collapse because of an instability.

BRIDGES

Engineers consider stiffness, strength, and stability when designing bridges. Bridges must be stiff because if they move, the movement might cause the bridge to fail. High strength will keep different parts of the bridge from breaking. Stability ensures that the bridge doesn't collapse.

There are many different types of bridges, but let's focus on two of the most common—beam bridges and **truss** bridges.

DID YOU KNOW?

Engineers design supports for artwork and sculptures in museums. These supports are especially important in areas where earthquakes happen frequently.

WORDS 2 KNOW

truss: a structure composed of slender **members** connected at the ends such that the members form strong triangles.

member: a component of a structure such as a truss member or beam.

17

structural: relating to the way something is built.

tension: a pulling force that pulls or stretches an object.

WORDS 2 KNOW

Beam bridges rely on a series of beams to support the load of the cars and trucks on the deck above. The first beam bridges were made by putting logs across creeks. Now, most beams are made from steel or concrete. Beam bridges are often used on highways for overpasses—look up the next time you go under one.

Beams are **structural** elements that resist bending under loads. When a group of cars passes over a beam bridge, the top of the beam compresses slightly. At the same time the underneath part of the beam stretches under **tension**.

The beam can only a hold a certain amount of weight. If the load becomes too heavy, the top of the beam will reach maximum compression while the bottom might snap from too much tension.

CABLE-STAYED AND SUSPENSION BRIDGES

Cable-stayed bridges and suspension bridges both rely on cable to support the deck. The main difference between the two types of bridges is that in a cable-stayed bridge, the cables used to support the deck are connected directly to the towers. In a suspension bridge, suspender cables transfer the load to the main cables, which are draped over the towers and connected to supports at the ends of the bridge.

How can engineers make sure this doesn't happen to their bridges? They choose an appropriate combination of **span**, size, and materials. Remember, a beam will be stiffer if it has a shape with more mass away from the central axis. This gives the beam a higher moment of inertia.

span: the distance between supports.

WORDS 2 KNOW

A truss is a structure made of triangles. Triangles tend to be very stable. The loads applied to a truss bridge are resisted by tension and compression in separate parts of the truss. Try building both a triangle and a rectangle using paper and paper fasteners or sticks and dowels. Then push on the forms. What happens? Which one is stiffer and more stable?

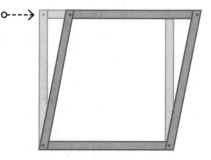

CONSIDER THE ESSENTIAL QUESTION

Write your thoughts about this chapter's Essential Question in your design journal, using information you've gathered from reading and knowledge you may already have. Share it with other students and friends. Did you all come up with the same answers? What is different? Do this for every chapter.

? ESSENTIAL QUESTION

How does an engineer design a structure to support a load?

DESIGN A STABILITY SCULPTURE

How do structures and sculptures differ? How are they similar? Sculptures are considered art, whereas structures typically serve a function—but both structures and sculptures must support loads and remain standing. How can you create a sculpture that looks unstable and beautiful but will remain standing?

1 Design Goal: Design and build a Stability Sculpture that is beautiful, can support the weight of one book, and has the greatest possible distance between the supports and the load. This will make it look unstable when it really isn't. Start by using only popsicle sticks, string, and hot glue.

2 Question: What will make your structure look unstable? How will you ensure it is stable? What types of supports will you use? How will you make the sculpture beautiful?

LEAN ON ME

The Leaning Tower of Pisa wasn't meant to be an oddity of architecture. It began to lean as the ground settled underneath the foundation soon after builders started work on it in 1173. Now, more than 800 years later, the Tower of Pisa has been stabilized thanks to different engineering solutions. The tower still leans, but its center of gravity falls within its base, so it won't collapse completely.

3 **Brainstorm:** Come up with lots of ideas. How can you create a sculpture that is beautiful but looks unstable? Sketch your ideas in your design journal.

4 **Select Alternatives:** Be sure to select alternatives that meet your design goals. Which ideas are the most likely to look beautiful yet unstable?

5 **Design and Prototype:** In the design and prototype phase, you will want to consider stiffness, strength, and stability. If your design is not stiff, there will be too much bending and maybe even breaking. When designing for strength, remember that you should consider the material and loading type. For example, string may be pulled but not pushed or bent. Stability, of course, will be a big factor in your design. Where will the center of gravity of the book be? Since your sculpture will include multiple members and may be connected at the base (rather than simply resting on the base) it will be okay if it lies outside of your supports. Building and testing prototypes will be the key to making sure the supports that you design are able to withstand the load of the book.

6 **Test and Reflect:** To test your designs, first make sure they meet your design goals. Can you place a book on your sculpture? How far is the book from the supports? Creativity and beauty can be a bit tougher to measure since everyone might have a different opinion. You can have friends and classmates judge your sculpture for creativity and beauty.

BUILD A CARDBOARD CHAIR

IDEAS FOR SUPPLIES:
cardboard ♦ 1 roll duct tape

Have you ever noticed that chairs come in all shapes and sizes? A chair needs to support the load of the person sitting in it without collapsing or tipping over. What else is important in the design of a chair?

1 **Design Goal:** Design a chair to support a person weighing up to 150 pounds using only cardboard and one roll of duct tape. The seat of the chair should be a minimum of 14 inches from the ground. The chair should have a back and be comfortable, and your design should be creative.

2 **Question:** How can you build a chair out of cardboard? What will make your chair comfortable? What are some fun chair designs you can try?

3 **Brainstorm:** Come up with LOTS of ideas. It is okay to look at existing chairs, but remember that one of your goals is to come up with a creative design.

CAN YOU TOUCH YOUR TOES?

Stand with your back, legs, and feet against a wall. Now try to touch your toes without holding on to anything or moving your feet. Can you do it? Why not? It is very difficult to touch your toes because your center of gravity is too far forward. And since you can't move your feet or legs, you are not able to readjust your center of gravity.

4 **Select Alternatives**: Be sure to select alternatives that meet your design goals— safety, comfort, and creativity.

5 **Design and Prototype:** During the design and prototype phase, consider stiffness, strength, and stability. Try building small-scale prototypes before building full-scale chairs.

Remember, if your design is not stiff, there will be too much **deflection** when you sit in it and the chair might collapse. Since your only material is cardboard, there is not too much you can do about strength, but test the cardboard to find a way for it to hold you. Stability will also be an issue. Make sure the chair won't be too easy to tip over, even when you lean on the back.

6 **Test and Reflect:** Test your design by sitting on it and leaning back. What happens? Be sure to measure the height of the seat. Is it at least 14 inches off the ground? Is the back of the chair a reasonable height to support your back comfortably? Does your chair support your weight without too much deflection? Is it comfortable? You might want to have a panel of judges evaluate comfort and creativity. Remember to reflect on your design. What worked? What didn't? What factors seem to affect strength, stiffness, and stability? What would you change about your original design?

CONSTRUCT A BEAM BRIDGE

IDEAS FOR SUPPLIES:

3 sheets paper, 11 by 17 inches ◆ 1 roll Scotch tape ◆ cardboard or foamcore, 6 inches by 15 inches ◆ Internet access ◆ pennies or small stones for the load

Many bridges that go over roads are beam bridges. Beam bridges are an efficient way to span a fairly short distance.

1 **Design Goal:** Create a beam bridge using three sheets of paper and one roll of Scotch tape. The bridge should span 15 inches and support the greatest possible load at the center. The bridge deck should be made of cardboard or foamcore.

2 **Question:** Ask an adult for permission to do some research on beam bridges online. What shapes are commonly used? Are the beams connected to the deck? How will your bridge be supported at the ends? How will the load be applied? How many beams should you use?

3 **Brainstorm:** Come up with LOTS of ideas. You might want to build and test as you brainstorm.

4 **Select Alternatives:** Be sure to select alternatives that meet your design goals.

5 **Design and Prototype:** In the design and prototype phase, you will want to consider stiffness, strength, and stability. If your design is not stiff, there will be too much deflection and too much bending, which will cause part of the bridge to break. Keep track of your designs in your design journal.

6 **Test and Reflect:** To test out your designs, elevate the ends of the bridge using books, bricks, chairs, or something else. The span of the bridge—in this case 15 inches—is the distance between the two supports on the sides. Test your beam bridge by placing a paper cup on the bridge deck and filling it with pennies or rocks until it breaks or collapses. How many pennies or how much weight did your bridge carry?

You could also measure the stiffness of your bridge by measuring the deflection of the bridge for a given amount of load. This will be less than the failure load. Remember to reflect on your designs. What worked? What didn't? What factors seem to affect strength, stiffness, and stability?

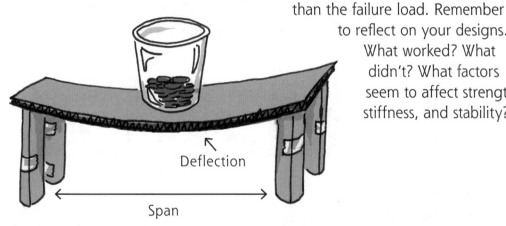

Deflection

Span

THE LONGEST BRIDGES

The longest bridge in the world is the Danyang–Kunshan Grand Bridge. Located in China, the bridge is 102.4 miles long. It is considered a viaduct, which is a type of beam bridge with short beams spanning between a series of columns.

The largest natural bridge in the world is the Xianren Bridge, also known as the Fairy Bridge, in northern Guangxi Province in China. The bridge was naturally formed from limestone karst, which is an area with a kind of rock called limestone. It spans 400 feet.

ENGINEER A TRUSS BRIDGE

IDEAS FOR SUPPLIES:

balsa wood ◆ paper ◆ hot glue gun ◆ cardboard or wood ◆ Internet access ◆ X-Acto knife or mini miter saw and box ◆ weights for the load

Truss bridges have been popular for railway bridges because they are able to carry large loads. Truss bridges are also typically used in wooden covered bridges. These bridges are covered to protect the wood of the trusses from weather.

1 **Design Goal:** Design a truss bridge that is able to span 10 inches and bear the most weight with the least amount of materials.

2 **Question:** Ask an adult for permission to do some research online. How are the members of trusses connected? What shapes are used?

3 **Brainstorm:** There are lots of options for arranging the triangles to create trusses. Take a look at these designs and decide which ones you want to build and test. Which shape is best for a 10-inch span?

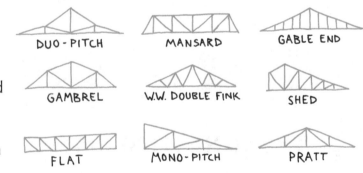

DUO-PITCH   MANSARD   GABLE END

GAMBREL   W.W. DOUBLE FINK   SHED

FLAT   MONO-PITCH   PRATT

4 **Select Alternatives:** Remember, you are not just building a bridge that can support the most load. You are trying to design the bridge with the highest strength-to-weight ratio. This means you want a bridge that can support a high load with the least amount of material, so you'll want to use the materials efficiently.

5 **Design and Prototype:** Your final prototype will be made of balsa wood, but first try building several prototypes out of paper or cardboard to test your ideas. Use a piece of wood or cardboard for the deck of the bridge. Remember, your bridge will be three-dimensional. Using triangles both vertically and horizontally will result in a stiffer and more stable bridge.

6 **Test and Reflect:** To test out your designs, elevate the ends of the bridge using books, bricks, chairs, or something else. Test your beam bridge by placing the load of bricks, books, or weights on the bridge deck or hanging them from below. Remember to weigh your bridge before you test it. To calculate the strength-to-weight ratio, divide the bridge's weight by the weight of the load it can carry. Add more weight until the bridge fails. Which design worked best? How might you improve your design?

STRONG CONNECTIONS

Building good connections between the truss members for your final prototype is very important. What might happen if those connections aren't strong enough? One of the strongest types of connections for a truss is a gusseted connection. A **gusset plate** is a sheet of material (paper, cardboard, or thin plywood in your case) that connect multiple members. Be sure to cut the members at the proper angle using an X-Acto knife or mini miter saw and box.

WORDS 2 KNOW

gusset plate: a sheet of material that is applied to the outside of multiple members to connect them.

Chapter 2
EVERYTHING IS SPINNING

**Engineers design and build many things that spin.
The wheels on bicycles and wheelchairs need to
spin to work. The propellers on boats and airplanes
and the blades on wind and water turbines are also
examples of things that need to spin to do their job.**

The scientific principles associated with spinning are used in many things, including the navigation systems on satellites and the electronics used to rotate the screen of an iPad or iPhone. What are some other examples of devices that rely on spinning?

? ESSENTIAL QUESTION

What factors affect the way something spins?

What would you like to build that spins? You can find the guidelines to these ideas at the end of the chapter.

- A race car that makes it to the bottom of the ramp fast!
- A spinning top that continues spinning the longest.
- An illusion machine that uses gears.

ROTATIONAL MOTION

DID YOU KNOW?

The earth spins slowly on a central axis, much like a spinning top. It rotates once about every 24 hours, resulting in day for the part of the earth facing the sun and night for the part of the earth facing away from the sun.

A central axis is an imaginary line through the center of an object. Can you find the North Pole and the South Pole on a globe? Imagine a real pole going all the way through the planet between the North and South Poles. That's the earth's central axis, and the earth rotates around this axis. When an object spins around a central axis, it has **rotational motion**.

To understand rotational motion, consider these questions. Will a ball travel faster down a smooth or a rough ramp? If two balls of different weights and sizes are released down a smooth ramp, which will reach the bottom first? What other factors affect rotational motion?

Get some marbles and set up a ramp with a board and books to test your ideas. Use a ruler as a starting gate to ensure the balls are released naturally, not pushed.

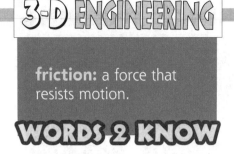

First, time how long it takes a marble to travel down the smooth ramp. Next, tape some sandpaper or create a series of bumps on the board by taping strips of cardboard to it. Time how long it takes the same marble to travel down this rough surface. What did you find?

Friction is a force that resists motion. It is one of the biggest factors affecting motion. Whenever one object comes in contact with another, such as the marble and the ramp, friction happens and slows the motion.

Have you ever tried rubbing your hand against sandpaper or used a skateboard on gravel?

The more contact between objects the more friction there is, and the harder it is for the objects to move against each other. Can you explain why the marble traveled faster down one surface of the ramp?

GALILEO AND MASS

Galileo was an Italian engineer and scientist who lived between 1564 and 1642. He was the first person to discover that two objects of the same mass fall at the same rates. More than 400 years ago, he tested his hypothesis by dropping objects from the Leaning Tower of Pisa. You can drop a bowling ball and a tennis ball from the same height and they will reach the ground at the same time, as long as factors such as air resistance or friction don't change the paths too much.

If two balls of different weights and sizes are released down a smooth ramp, which will make it to the bottom first? Use your starting gate to release two marbles, one larger than the other, down the ramp at the same time. What did you find? Are you surprised?

**Higher
moment of inertia**
(rolls slower)

What other factors affect rotational motion? Take the lid from a jar and tape pennies evenly around the outer edge of the lid. Record the amount of time it takes the lid to roll down your smooth ramp.

Now tape the pennies all stacked together at the center of the lid. Record the amount of time it takes the lid to travel down your smooth ramp. What did you find? Which one traveled faster?

Remember when we talked about the moment of inertia? We learned that an I-beam, which has more of its mass farther from the center, has a higher moment of inertia than a rectangular beam. The I-beam is stiffer, or deflects less.

**Lower
moment of inertia**
(rolls faster)

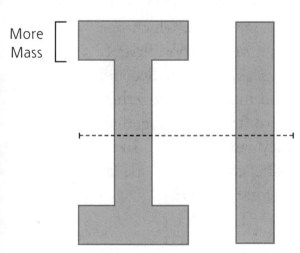

More
Mass

The same principle applies to a **cylindrical** object that has more of its mass farther from the center and a higher moment of inertia. The lid with the pennies taped around the outer edge has a higher moment of inertia than the lid with the pennies taped in the center. A higher moment of inertia makes the object rotate more slowly.

WORDS 2 KNOW

cylindrical: round.

31

WORDS 2 KNOW

analog: presenting data as a measurable physical quality, not as numbers.

transmit: to send or pass something from one place or person to another.

power: energy used through time.

energy: the ability to do work or cause change.

windmill: a device that converts the energy of the wind to mechanical energy.

Have you even spun on ice skates or roller skates with your arms out wide, and then tucked your arms in closer to your body? What happens? You spin faster when you bring your arms closer to your body. Why? What are you doing to your moment of inertia?

GEARS

What do you see if you look at the inside of an **analog** clock? All of those tiny gears make the hands move around the face and keep time. How do the gears do this?

Gears are used in many devices, including cars, bicycles, clocks, and wind turbines. Why do engineers use gears? Gears enable us do several things, such as **transmit power**, change the direction of rotation, and change the speed of a rotating object. Let's focus on using gears to change the speed of rotation.

DID YOU KNOW!

Ancient gears were built out of wood and were used in **windmills,** waterwheels, and winches. Winches are mechanical devices used to tighten ropes and cables.

If two cylinders of different sizes rotate at the same speed, which one will complete a full rotation first? If we take two gears, one smaller and one larger, and mesh them together, they will have to rotate together, right? If they are different sizes, will they rotate at the same speed? Or will one rotate faster?

Since the gears mesh together, they will have to travel the same distance. When the gear with the smaller **circumference** has made a full **revolution**, the gear with the larger circumference will only have rotated part way around. Which one will appear to be spinning faster? In this case, the smaller one.

Cut out two circles of different circumferences from a piece of paper. Wrap a string once around the smaller circle, and then see how far that same length of string is able to wrap around the larger circle. Imagine the string wraps halfway around the larger circle. That would mean the larger gear spins half as fast as the smaller one.

The **gear ratio** is the ratio of the speed of one gear to another. It is a function of the **radius** of each gear. The radius of the gear is the measurement from the center of the gear to the outside edge of the gear. If the radius of one gear is twice as large as the radius of another gear, the gear ratio would be 2:1, or 1:2, depending on which gear is causing the motion and which is being moved.

circumference: the distance around the edge of a circle.

revolution: one complete turn made by something moving in a circle around a fixed point.

gear ratio: the rate the first gear rotates divided by the rate the last gear rotates.

radius: the distance from the center of a circle to the outside edge of the circle.

WORDS 2 KNOW

Radius = 1
Radius = 2
Gear Ratio = 1:2

? ESSENTIAL QUESTION

Now it's time to consider and discuss the Essential Question: What factors affect the way something spins?

RACE CAR

Engineers continue to improve the design of cars and other vehicles to make them more efficient and able to travel farther and faster.

1 **Design Goal:** Design a race car that travels the fastest down a smooth ramp. Your race car may be designed using the materials of your choice but must include at least four different parts.

2 **Question:** Should your car be big or small? Remember what you learned about rotational motion. Does the mass and size of the car affect the speed? What else could affect the speed?

3 **Brainstorm:** Come up with LOTS of ideas. Search for fun and creative materials to use for your car. Keep track of your research and ideas in your design journal.

BICYCLES USE GEARS THAT SPIN

One of the first two-wheeled machines, called the draisine, was invented in 1817 by Karl von Drais, a German baron. The draisine did not have pedals and was moved forward by pushing your feet on the ground. The first two-wheeled bicycle to use gears and a chain drive was invented in France in the early 1860s.

4 **Select Alternatives:** Be sure to select alternatives that meet your design goal of being fast!

5 **Design and Prototype:** Friction will play a big role in the speed of your race car. You have experimented with the speed of balls on a smooth ramp versus a rough ramp to demonstrate friction. But friction can also occur when parts of your car rub together. The friction caused by parts rubbing together will slow down your car. When constructing your car, try to minimize all sources of friction.

6 **Test and Reflect:** Test your race car by releasing it down a ramp. Remember to release the car instead of pushing it. What worked in your design? What didn't? What factors affected the speed of your race car? How might you design your car differently?

SPINNING TOP

Spinning toys come in many different forms. The world's largest spinning top is 30 feet tall! It's a sculpture by artist Peter Hohmann, located in Oosterhout in the Netherlands. What sizes, forms, and designs result in a spinning motion that lasts a long time?

1 **Design Goal:** Design a spinning top that spins for the longest amount of time.

2 **Question:** How will you design your spinning top? How does the shape of the spinner affect the performance? Should the stem of your top go through the center of the body or should it be off center? Is it better to design a spinning top with a large or small diameter? Is it better to have a heavier or lighter spinning top? How about handle height versus tip height? Is it better to have the body of the spinning top close to the tip or higher up? Should the tip be pointed or rounded? How does weight distribution affect performance? Is it better if the weight is closer to the center or farther away from the center?

"Art without engineering is dreaming. Engineering without art is calculating."

—**Steven Roberts, engineer who travels the world in transportation of his own design**

3 **Brainstorm:** Come up with LOTS of ideas. What shapes will you use? How many layers will you use? Will your body be solid or include openings?

4 Select Alternatives: You might need to experiment with spinning tops of different designs before selecting alternatives. Record your designs in your design journal.

5 Design and Prototype: Construction quality will be an important factor in how well your top spins. Create a good connection between the body and the stem using glue, tape, or clay. Be careful when cutting out the body of your spinning top: the hole in the body should be through the center of gravity to ensure your top is balanced. Use a craft knife or circle cutter to cut out the body of your top to make it balanced and **symmetrical**. The body of the top can be composed of multiple layers of cardboard or foamcore. Decorate your spinning top if you wish.

6 Test and Reflect: Now for the fun part—spinning your top! The speed at which you spin the top initially is a factor so try to be consistent with how you spin it. Getting the top started can be a bit of an art so you may need to practice. How long can you keep your top spinning? How could you improve your design?

DID YOU KNOW?

A gyroscope is a type of spinning top that was a popular toy in the early 1900s. Gyroscopes are still available as spinning toys but they are also used in many engineered devices, including satellites, compasses, and iPhones.

SPINNING ILLUSION MACHINE

A spinning toy called a **thaumatrope** was popular in the nineteenth century. Part of an image is drawn on one side of a disk and the other part of the image is drawn on the other side. When you spin the disk fast enough, the images come together to create the illusion that they are a single image. A picture of a bird on one side and a cage on the other would blur together to look like a bird in a cage. This is an example of an **optical illusion**.

DID YOU KNOW?

Engineers can create the illusion of motion by taking a series of still images that vary only slightly from one another and rapidly displaying them in sequence. Many movies are animated using a similar process, including *The Lion King*, *Aladdin*, and *The Lord of the Rings*.

1 **Design Goal:** Make a modern-day thaumatrope by designing a machine that rotates at a speed high enough to create an optical illusion.

2 **Question:** What images will you use for your thaumatrope? What speed is required to create an optical illusion? How can you cause something to spin fast enough to create an optical illusion? What gear ratio do you need to use? Sketch some ideas in your design journal.

WORDS 2 KNOW

thaumatrope: a popular nineteenth-century spinning toy.

optical illusion: a trick of the eyes that makes people see something differently than it really is.

FRONT

BACK

3 Brainstorm and Select Alternatives: For this activity you might want to jump right in and start playing with spools, dowels, and rubber bands—brainstorm as you build! Your selection will depend on what works.

4 Design and Prototype: First experiment with gears. Start by mounting two spools onto a board using nails or dowels. Stretch a rubber band between these two gears. Rotate one of the spools and see what happens to the other. In this scenario, you'll want to use the gears to increase the speed of rotation. Will you want to rotate the smaller or larger spool by hand? You may want to build a handle for the input gear using a dowel or foamcore. Continue to experiment with gears by using spools of different sizes and adding more gears. Can you design a **gear train** with three or more gears? Once you are happy with your design, mount your thaumatrope on the fastest spinning gear to create your optical illusion.

5 Test and Reflect: What worked? What didn't? What gear ratios did you use? How might you improve your design?

39

Chapter 3
STAYING AFLOAT AND ALOFT

What do air and water have in common? While they might seem very different, water and air are both fluids that have many of the same characteristics. We can design objects to stay afloat in water and aloft in the air using the principles of buoyancy, lift, and drag.

WORDS 2 KNOW

fluid: a **substance** such as a gas or a liquid that flows freely and has no fixed shape.

substance: matter with specific properties.

buoyancy: the upward force from a fluid that helps an object float.

lift: an upward force due to the motion of an object through the air.

drag: a force that acts to slow down an object in air.

? **ESSENTIAL QUESTION**

How does buoyancy help you float? How does lift help keep an airplane aloft?

flink: a combination of floating and sinking. When something flinks it **hovers** in the water.

hover: to float without moving.

Engineers study fluids when they design and build airplanes, boats, turbines, parachutes, and much more. What would you like to design that floats or flies? Here are a few ideas for projects, with guidelines at the end of the chapter. What other ideas do you have?

- A thingamajig that **flinks**!

- A buoy with a funny use.

- A parachute to safely drop heavy, sensitive supplies into a small target zone.

- Your own hot air balloon!

BUOYANCY IN WATER

Can you pull or push on water or air? Pulling on water or air might not be possible, but pushing certainly is. What happens when you push down on water in the sink, a pool, or a lake?

Fill your bathroom sink with water and push down on the surface with your hand. Can you feel the water pushing back on your hand even as it flows out of your way? This upward force pushing on your hand is known as buoyancy. Buoyancy is the upward force from a fluid that helps an object float.

Buoyancy from the water helps support people and things. Buoyancy also helps you float when you are swimming.

Try putting a lump of clay into a cup of water. What happens to the clay? Because clay is heavy, the force of the clay on the water is greater than the force of the water on the clay. Buoyancy doesn't help much to keep the clay afloat!

What happens if you change the shape of the clay? Can you find a shape that allows it to float, or is the weight of the clay just too much no matter what the shape? Shape the clay into a boat and place it back in the water. Do you get a different result?

Buoyancy depends on how much water is displaced by an object.

ARCHIMEDES' PRINCIPLE

Legend says that Archimedes was asked by the king to determine whether his crown was made of pure gold or a material of lesser quality. While taking a bath, Archimedes had a brilliant idea. He noticed that the water in the bathtub rose when he got in. He hypothesized that the volume of water displaced was equal to the volume of his body. He determined the volume of the king's crown by measuring the amount of water displaced when it was submerged. When he measured the weight of equal volumes of different materials Archimedes was able to determine that the crown was NOT made of pure gold! You can watch a video about his discovery.

video Archimedes' discovery

42

The lump of clay only displaces a small **volume** of water, while a boat-shaped piece of clay displaces a larger volume of water. Volume is the amount of space an object takes up.

Depth
1 inch

Height
1 inch

Volume
1 inch³

Width
1 inch

Consider a cube of clay that is 1 inch on each side. The cube has a volume of 1 inch cubed, written as 1 inch³. You find this volume by multiplying 1 inch by 1 inch by 1 inch.

Volume = Height × Width × Depth
1 inch³ = 1 inch × 1 inch × 1 inch

When you change the shape of the cube to create an open box, you might make an object with a base that is 2 inches by 2 inches with a height of 2 inches. This box can displace a volume of water that is 2 inches by 2 inches by 2 inches, or 8 inches³. 1 inch³ is less than 8 inches³. The open box can displace eight times as much water as the cube.

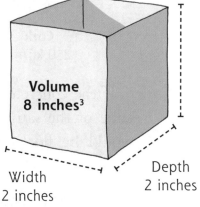

Height
2 inches

Volume
8 inches³

Width
2 inches

Depth
2 inches

How does the amount of water displaced relate to buoyancy? The buoyancy force equals the weight of the displaced water. If the buoyancy force is greater than the weight of the object, the object will float. And if the buoyancy force is less than the weight of the object, it will sink.

"From birth, man carries the weight of gravity on his shoulders. He is bolted to earth. But man has only to sink beneath the surface and he is free. Buoyed by water, he can fly in any direction—up, down, sideways—by merely flipping his hand."

—Jacques-Yves Cousteau, undersea explorer

More volume = more buoyant force!

density: the amount of matter in a given space, or mass divided by volume.

WORDS 2 KNOW

If the open box made of clay displaces enough water that the buoyancy force is greater than the weight of the clay, the open box will float!

Density is also a factor in determining whether an object will float or sink. Let's consider four cubes of identical size but of different materials and densities—cork, wood, concrete, and gold. Which of these objects do you expect to float? Why?

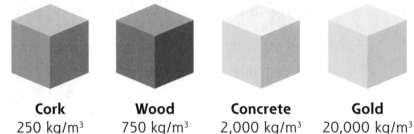

| **Cork** | **Wood** | **Concrete** | **Gold** |
| 250 kg/m³ | 750 kg/m³ | 2,000 kg/m³ | 20,000 kg/m³ |

If the concrete cube is just submerged, only two-thirds of a wood cube of the same size would be submerged. Most of the cork cube would be floating on the surface. The gold cube will be on the bottom of the pond.

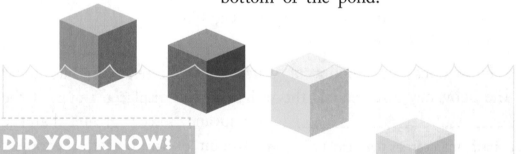

DID YOU KNOW?

College students have been designing, building, and racing concrete canoes for many years.

Now let's take those same four materials—cork, wood, concrete, and gold—and vary their sizes so that they all float at the same level. How large do the different cubes need to be to make this happen?

Using the same densities for the materials as in the previous example and using cork as the baseline, the wood needs to have base dimensions that are 1.7 times larger, concrete would need to be 2.8 times larger, and gold would need to be 8.9 times larger.

BUOYANCY IN THE AIR

Buoyancy in the air works in the same way as buoyancy in water. If the buoyancy force is greater than the weight of the object, the object will float. If the buoyancy force is less than the weight of the object, it will sink.

Compare a balloon filled with helium with a balloon filled with air. What happens to the one filled with air? The one filled with helium? Objects that weigh more than air will sink and objects that weigh less than air will float. If you fill a balloon with air, it will not float, but if you fill it with helium, it will. That is because helium weighs about seven times less than air, making it a great gas to use for birthday balloons.

Have you ever seen a hot air balloon travel over land? Hot air balloons are equipped with burners that heat the air inside the balloons. Hot air weighs less than cooler air, so the balloon rises.

GLIDERS AND AIRPLANES

What about gliders, airplanes, and other flying objects? What keeps them aloft? Buoyant forces still apply to airplanes, but unless we filled planes with helium, buoyancy won't be much help in keeping a plane aloft! Instead, a lift force is at work.

While a lift force has some similarities to a buoyant force, there is one big difference. A lift force, which acts upward on the wings of the plane, requires that the plane be moving. Differences in the speed and pressure of the air above and below the wing cause a lift force. Usually, the larger the area of the wings, the stronger the lift force.

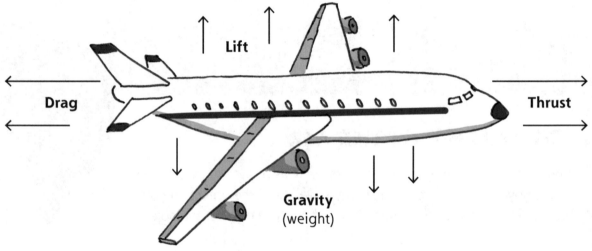

A drag force acts in the opposite direction of the motion of the plane.

Drag tries to slow down the motion. Have you ever tried to walk through deep water? The friction of the water keeps you from moving very fast. Air acts the same way on a plane and creates drag. Planes and cars and many other moving objects are designed to reduce the amount of drag force.

molecule: a group of atoms bound together. Molecules combine to form matter.

WORDS 2 KNOW

Other objects, such as parachutes, rely on drag to slow the speed of a falling object. When engineers design a parachute, they try to maximize the drag force. Drag is really just air resistance. It is a way of slowing down objects.

If you drop a rock and a feather from a tree house window, which will fall to the ground the fastest? The laws of gravity state that gravity exerts the same force on all objects, no matter the difference in mass. But there is a big difference in the air resistance, or drag, on each object. Air **molecules** are pushing on the feather and the rock as they fall, which slows down the motion. The feather has a larger surface for the air molecules to hit, so the feather slows more than the rock.

If you were designing a parachute, how would you maximize the drag? Should the material be heavy or light? Should the parachute be large or small? Think about the feather. Should you design a parachute like a feather?

Engineers use the principles of drag, buoyancy, and lift when they design airplanes, gliders, cars, parachutes, and many other things. Understanding and applying these principles helps engineers predict the behavior of their different designs without having to test every different option. For example, they can predict the size of the wings needed on an airplane by balancing the weight, lift, and drag forces.

? ESSENTIAL QUESTION

Now it's time to consider and discuss the Essential Question: How does buoyancy help you float? How does lift help keep an airplane aloft?

FLINKING THINGAMAJIG

**Objects float because they are less dense than water or shaped
in a way that they displace enough water. What about an object
that neither floats on top of the water nor sinks to the bottom?
An object that flinks will hover somewhere below the surface.**

1 **Design Goal:** Design a thingamajig that flinks. You want it to hover
below the surface of the water.

2 **Question:** Why do objects sink? Why do they float? How will you
balance these two opposing behaviors? There are really no rules on how
you accomplish this goal!

3 **Brainstorm:** Come up with LOTS of
ideas—the crazier the better for the design
of your thingamajig.

4 **Select Alternatives:** Remember
your design goal of creating a
thingamajig that neither sinks nor floats!

DID YOU KNOW?

**Submarines must be able to both
float and stay submerged. To
adjust the level of a submarine,
seawater is let in and out
of the submarine to adjust
its weight and elevation.**

5 **Design and Prototype:** Test your objects to learn more about what floats and what sinks, then combine them to create something that flinks.

6 **Test and Reflect:** Time how long you are able to flink your thingamajig. Reflect on your design. What worked? What didn't work? What factors affect how long your thingamajig was able to flink?

THE STORY OF THE TITANIC

The *RMS Titanic* was supposed to be the world's first unsinkable ship, but it sank on its very first voyage in April 1912 after hitting an **iceberg**. The iceberg caused damage to the **hull** of the ship and water came aboard, which made the *Titanic* heavier and caused it to sink.

It went fully underwater when the total weight of the ship and the water in it was greater than the buoyant force of the water beneath the ship. It happened in the same way as when you're doing the dishes in the sink and the cup you're washing fills with water and suddenly sinks. It took less than three hours for the *Titanic* to sink after hitting the iceberg.

Did you know you can use Archimedes' principle to help explain what happened to the *Titanic*?

Archimedes' principle Titanic 🔍

WORDS 2 KNOW

iceberg: a large piece of floating ice.

hull: the body of a ship.

49

CUSTOM-DESIGNED BUOY

Buoys are floating devices used to help boats navigate, mark a location, collect data, communicate, and much more. Buoys can be anchored or allowed to drift.

1 **Design Goal:** Design a buoy that floats, is able to withstand a wind load, is as tall as possible, and may be used creatively. You get to decide what your buoy will do! Maybe it will warn or welcome boaters and swimmers or support a basketball hoop. What other ideas can you come up with? Keep track of them in your design journal.

2 **Question:** How will you create a tall buoy that is able to float and support a force pushing on it, maybe from the wind or from a ship hitting it? Consider buoyancy and density. With an adult's permission, do some research online. How are buoys designed?

3 **Brainstorm:** What might be some fun applications for a buoy? Remember to come up with LOTS of ideas, even crazy ones. How will you build your buoy? What materials will you use?

4 **Select Alternatives:** Which ideas are the most creative? Which ideas will meet the goal of your buoy being tall, able to float, and able to resist a wind load?

DID YOU KNOW?

The longest floating bridge in the world is located near Seattle, Washington. It carries traffic across Lake Washington.

WORDS 2 KNOW

drift: to move freely on the water.

5 **Design and Prototype:** Test and build lots of prototypes. Be sure to push horizontally on your buoy to see if it is able to resist a horizontal load and return to standing.

6 **Test and Reflect:** Test your buoy by placing it in water to see if it floats. Push on it horizontally to see if is able to stay afloat. Is your use of the buoy creative? What worked with your design? What could be improved?

ICE WATER SCIENCE

Why does ice float? Isn't ice heavier than water? Actually, when water freezes into ice, it expands and becomes less dense and lighter. Icebergs are really just giant, floating ice cubes.

Check out this simulation to play more with density and buoyancy. Why do some squares sink and other materials float? What do you know about their volumes and densities?

density buoyancy simulation 🔍

SUPPLY PARACHUTE

Ideas for supplies:

pennies ◆ plastic bags ◆ tissue paper ◆ cardboard ◆ paper ◆ string ◆ glue ◆ tape

Imagine the following scenario: A group of students is stranded in a remote mountain village that's been hit with a major snowstorm. The only way to get them supplies is to use a parachute. The supplies needed include sensitive communication equipment that is heavy and fragile. You also need to think about where your supplies can land, as the area is mountainous— and missing the target might mean losing the supplies.

1 Design Goal: Design a specialized parachute to deliver its load precisely and carefully. Your parachute must be able to carry as many pennies as possible and land as closely as possible to the target.

2 Question: How will you design your parachute? How large should you make it? What materials will you use? How will you ensure that the parachute hits the target without toppling over? From what height will you release your parachute?

3 Brainstorm and Select Alternatives: Experiment with different materials and sizes for your parachute to find out what works and what doesn't. You'll need to balance the weight carried with the speed of your descent. Write down your ideas in your design journal.

DID YOU KNOW?

The Sherpa is a GPS-supported, remote-controlled parachute used by the United States military and Special Forces. It delivers cargo and helps with search-and-rescue missions. Some versions of the Sherpa can safely deliver up to 10,000 pounds of cargo to the ground.

4 **Design and Prototype:** Build parachutes of different sizes using different materials to test out your ideas.

5 **Test and Reflect:** Test your parachute by releasing it from a specified height, such as from a window, balcony, or ladder. Set up a target so you can determine whether your parachute lands in the correct spot or not. Remember that you want a soft landing so the cargo will be safe. After you test your parachute, reflect on your design. How could you improve your parachute?

MARS ROVER *CURIOSITY*

A special parachute was designed for the Mars Rover *Curiosity*, which landed on Mars in 2012. Even though *Curiosity* is a huge and heavy rover, it landed safely and within 1.5 miles of the planned target.

coolest Mars landing 🔎   Mars Rover Curiosity 🔎

HOT AIR BALLOON

IDEAS FOR SUPPLIES:
hair dryer ♦ *plastic bag or tissue paper* ♦ *glue stick or scotch tape* ♦ *pipe cleaners*

Humans first flew using hot air balloons, many years before the airplane was invented. That first flight took place in Paris, France, in 1783. An American and a Russian traveled 7,000 miles from Japan to Mexico in January 2015, successfully crossing the Pacific Ocean in a helium-filled hot air balloon.

1 **Design Goal:** Design a hot air balloon that stays aloft for the longest amount of time. Do some planning in your design journal.

2 **Question:** How will you design your hot air balloon? How large can you make it? What materials can you use to build your balloon?

3 **Brainstorm and Select Alternatives:** Experiment with different materials and sizes for your balloon to find out what works and what doesn't work. Remember that weight is a factor. Should you use heavy materials to build your balloon?

4 **Design and Prototype:** Construction quality will be an important part of your balloon's success. The bottom of the balloon can remain open, but the sides and top should be sealed. Test lots of ideas.

5 **Test and Reflect:** Use a hairdryer to heat up the air in your balloon. Does your balloon rise in the air? How long does it stay aloft? How could you improve your design?

Chapter 4
QUITE THE REACTION

Have you ever put water in the freezer to make ice cubes or boiled it to make a cup of hot cocoa? Do you wash your hands with soap? Do you put on sunscreen when you go to the beach? If you answered yes to any of these questions, then you've observed chemistry in action.

What would you like to design and build that relies on chemical reactions? Some ideas to get you started are on the next page. You can find guidelines at the end of the chapter.

What would life be like without the **phase** changes of matter? If water never turned to snow or ice or steam? If milk never turned to ice cream?!

WORDS 2 KNOW

chemistry: the study of how matter changes.

phase: the physical form that matter takes, such as a solid, liquid, or gas. Also called states of matter.

- A snow globe with snowflakes.
- A reaction large enough to launch a rocket.
- A recipe to make a bouncing ball.

Chemistry is the study of matter and how it changes. Matter is something that has mass. It can be a solid, a liquid, or a gas, and matter can change from one of these phases to another—and back again.

Matter is composed of **atoms**, which are the smallest particles of any substance. You are made of matter. So is the chair you sit on, the book or tablet you read, the water you drink, and the air you breath.

Chemistry is happening all around us. When you wear your raincoat on a rainy day, it is chemistry that made that water-repellent fabric. Do you take medicine when you have a bad headache? Thank chemistry! The fuels that are used to heat your home and run the family car are also possible because of chemistry. Even your smartphone, tablet, and MP3 player are made possible through chemistry.

Chemical engineers were involved in the development of all of these products. These engineers apply chemistry and

DID YOU KNOW?

Chemical engineers hold a variety of jobs—creating new medicines, better-tasting foods, new types of fuels, new fabrics for clothing, and many other products that you use every day.

other science and math principles while working with matter in different phases. They use **mixtures** and **chemical reactions** to solve problems and design new products and processes.

PHASES OF MATTER

One way that matter changes is by altering its phase or state. A phase or state is the form that matter takes. In this book, we'll focus on three phases of matter—liquids, solids, and gases.

Consider water. Have you ever heard water called H_2O? This means that a water molecule is made of two hydrogen atoms and one oxygen atom. Water is made of lots and lots of water molecules. Water is the liquid form of H_2O.

Hydrogen (+)

Oxygen (−)

When water freezes, it becomes ice, which is the solid form of H_2O.

This is an example of a change of phase from liquid to solid. Water freezes or melts at a temperature of 32 degrees Fahrenheit (0 degrees Celsius).

SALTY ICE

During winter in cold climates, trucks spread salt on the road. Salt and water combine to form a solution that freezes at a lower temperature. This is known as freezing-point depression. A lower freezing point on the roads means ice may not form, which makes it safer for driving. The freezing-point depression also helps explain why the salt water in the ocean takes longer to freeze than the freshwater in a lake.

When water boils, it changes to steam, which is the gas phase of H_2O. This is an example of a change of phase from liquid to gas. Water becomes steam at a temperature of 212 degrees Fahrenheit (100 degrees Celsius).

These changes in the water's phases from solid to liquid to gas are changes in the physical state of the water. The water changes physically but does not change chemically. It's always H_2O. Physical changes result from changes in temperature, pressure, and other physical means.

GAS, LIQUID, SOLID

What is the difference between a gas, a liquid, and a solid? A gas is a state or phase of matter with its molecules freely moving around in all directions. It does not have a shape and will spread out to fill a solid container. It can also be compressed into a very small container. A liquid is a state of matter with its molecules loosely packed together. A liquid flows to take the shape of its solid container. A solid is a state of matter where the molecules are bound tightly. A solid has a definite shape and volume and does not flow.

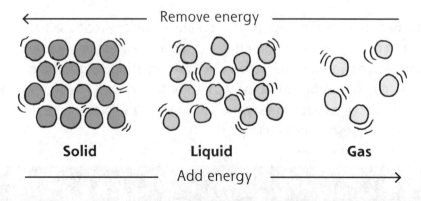

Water, ice, and steam are all made up of hydrogen and oxygen atoms, but the densities of these atoms change in each phase. Density is mass per unit volume, or the amount of matter in a given space. To change from a solid to a liquid to a gas, you need to add energy, such as heat. To change from a gas to a liquid to a solid, you need to take energy away.

Usually, the solid state of matter is the densest, followed by the liquid state, with gas being the least dense. Think of a room full of kids doing jumping jacks. In a small room, they wouldn't have much space and might not be able to raise their arms up very high without hitting someone else. In a larger room, such as a gymnasium, there would be plenty of room for everyone to spread out and have lots of space. And if the walls of the gymnasium

suddenly disappeared, kids could move way out and never even come near each other while they did their jumping jacks. The small room full of kids is like a solid, the gymnasium full of kids is like a liquid, and the kids outside are like a gas.

Water is an exception to the density rule. Solid water is actually less dense than liquid water, which is why the ice cubes in your glass of water float. The atoms in water freeze with more space between them than in the liquid form.

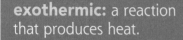
Engineers use and apply the principles of phase changes when they design and build many products and processes.

One key area that relies heavily on phase changes is steam turbines. These are rotating mechanical devices used to convert mechanical energy to electricity. In steam turbines, water is heated to produce steam. The steam is used to rotate turbines to produce electricity.

Engineers also rely on phase changes to develop products and processes that store and release heat. One example is hand warmers, which are used in cold climates. Some hand warmers rely on a chemical reaction, but others use phase changes. As the material in a hand warmer is warmed, it turns to liquid and stores heat. As it cools and changes back to a solid, it releases that heat, which can be used to warm your hands.

MIXTURES AND SOLUTIONS

What happens if you mix sand in water? How about salt in water? What is the same about these two mixtures? What is different?

Sand in water is an example of a mixture. A mixture is the physical combination of two or more things where no chemical reaction occurs. Sand and water can be mixed but neither of them changes into a different kind of matter. The sand will eventually settle to the bottom. Trail mix is another example of a mixture. You can easily separate the different nuts, chocolate, and granola.

Mixture
(no chemical change)

Solution
(chemical change)

A **solution**, on the other hand, is the chemical combination of two or more things. When you mix salt in water, the salt **dissolves**. There is a chemical change. In this case, the salt is considered the **solute** and the water is the **solvent**.

What happens when you mix powdered cocoa into warm water or milk? The cocoa powder dissolves in the water, forming a new solution—hot cocoa. If you add too much powder, you'll end up with extra powder in the bottom of your cup. Solvents can only dissolve a certain amount of a solute. Once a solvent reaches the point where it can no longer dissolve any more solute, it is said to be **saturated**.

Experiment with different substances to see which combinations form mixtures and which form solutions. What happens when you mix salt and pepper? Water and lemon juice? Chemical engineers use solutions and mixtures when they design medicine, food, and cleaning supplies.

CHOCOLATE ENGINEERING

You might not expect engineering to play a role in the chocolate you eat, but chemical engineers work with candy and chocolate companies to improve the quality of chocolate. Engineers vary the quality and texture of chocolate by experimenting with different chocolate "solutions" made of cacao, butter, milk, and sugar.

photosynthesis: the process through which plants change carbon dioxide, water, and light into glucose and oxygen.

carbon dioxide: a gas in the air made of carbon and oxygen atoms.

glucose: a type of sugar a plant makes for food.

WORDS 2 KNOW

REACTIONS

Combining two or more substances might result in a chemical reaction. When a chemical reaction takes place, something completely new is formed. **Photosynthesis,** rust, fire, and digestion, are all examples of chemical reactions.

During photosynthesis, plants change **carbon dioxide**, water, and light into **glucose** and oxygen. Humans and animals breathe in oxygen and release carbon dioxide. Plants absorb carbon dioxide and release oxygen.

That's why it's important to limit the number of trees we cut down. We need trees to use our carbon dioxide and give us oxygen.

Rust and fire are also examples of chemical reactions. Rust occurs when iron combines with oxygen and water to form iron oxide, the official name for rust. A fire from a campfire, candle, or match is the reaction between a hydrocarbon (often fuel or wood) and oxygen, which forms water, carbon dioxide, and energy, usually in the form of heat.

Lots of chemicals are at work in your body digesting your food, which is just another type of chemical reaction. The energy in the food is converted to energy that your body can use.

We use chemical reactions many times every day without even realizing it.

What happens when you wash your hands? The chemicals in the soap combine with dirt and oil on your hands to help lift these substances away from your skin. This chemical reaction gets your hands clean!

Chemical reactions may happen fast, as with a fire, or slow, as with rusting. They may be explosive, such as when rocket fuel is lit on fire, or quiet, as when you digest your food. They may be exothermic, meaning that they produce heat. Or they may be **endothermic**, meaning they absorb heat.

WORDS 2 KNOW

endothermic: a reaction that absorbs heat.

COOKING WITH CHEMISTRY

Cooking is a form of chemical engineering. By mixing different ingredients together you are creating chemical mixtures, solutions, and reactions. Adding heat may change the reaction rate or composition of whatever you are cooking. Changing a recipe to meet your specific tastes is a form of engineering.

Baking soda combined with moisture and an acidic ingredient forms a reaction that produces carbon dioxide when heated. The result is that cookies, cakes, and other yummy treats rise as the carbon dioxide bubbles form. This is an example of a fast-acting reaction. Once you mix in the baking soda, you should get your cookies in the oven quickly! What might happen if you wait too long?

Do you wear a raincoat when you go outside on a wet day? Chemical engineers used their knowledge about chemical reactions to create new fabrics that are strong and water repellent. What did you have for lunch? There's a good chance a chemical engineer worked with different chemical reactions to create that exact flavor. Chemical engineers are working in nearly every industry to create or improve on the experiences we have in the world.

DID YOU KNOW?

Gore-tex is a waterproof but breathable fabric that was invented by a chemical engineer named Bob Gore.

? ESSENTIAL QUESTION

Now it's time to consider and discuss the Essential Question: What would life be like without phase changes? If water never turned to snow or ice or steam? If milk never turned to ice cream?!

SNOW GLOBE

Ideas for Supplies:
clear jar with a screw lid ♦ solutes (glitter, salt, sugar, powder, sand, cornstarch, and borax) ♦ solvents (water, vegetable oil, mineral oil, and glycerin)

By designing and building a snow globe, you get to be crafty while learning about solutions and mixtures.

1 **Design Goal:** Design a snow globe with snowflakes that drift as slowly as possible to the bottom when you shake it.

2 **Question:** How will you create snowflakes? Will you create a saturated solution? Or will you use a solute that doesn't dissolve in your solvent? Which solutes dissolve in the solvents you have? Which do not?

3 **Brainstorm:** You might want to spend some time experimenting with mixtures and solutions before you build.

4 **Select Alternatives:** Select the solution that has snowflakes that are the size and density you like that drift slowly to the bottom when you shake the jar.

5 **Design and Prototype:** To build your prototype, glue decorations or small figurines to the lid of the jar (hot glue works best). Then fill the jar with the solvent and solute of your choice and screw the lid back on.

6 **Test and Reflect:** Test your snow globe by shaking it and timing the snowflakes as they drift to the bottom. Reflect on your design. What worked? What didn't? What factors affect the rate at which the snowflakes drift to the bottom? How could you make your snow globe better?

REACTION ROCKET

SAFETY TIP: Have an adult help you with this activity and always wear eye protection.

The chemical reaction between an antacid such as Alka-Seltzer and water or vinegar is an example of a fast-acting reaction that can be explosive. The whole idea is to produce an explosive reaction to model the thrust of a rocket. As the reaction pushes the lid of the rocket off, the rocket should move the other way. This is an example of Newton's third law of motion, which states that for every action there is an equal and opposite reaction.

① **Design Goal:** Create a reaction that launches a rocket into the air. Do some planning in your design journal.

② **Question:** How much of each solvent and solute will you use? How quickly will the reaction take place? What happens as you change the amount of solute per unit of solvent? How will you decorate your rocket to make it look good but also to be more **aerodynamic**?

③ **Brainstorm:** Take notes on all of your trials. Start with a small amount of solute in your solvent of choice (say, a quarter of an Alka-Seltzer tablet or ¼ teaspoon of cornstarch in ⅛ cup of water). You can slow the reaction time by wrapping your solute in a small amount of tissue paper. Be sure to place the film canister with the lid face down on your launch pad so the thrust produced causes the rocket to be propelled upward.

WORDS 2 KNOW

aerodynamic: having a shape that reduces the amount of drag when moving through the air or water, enabling a shape to move quickly through the air or water.

4 **Select Alternatives:** Select the solute-and-solvent ratio that gives you a reasonable reaction time but launches your rocket the highest.

5 **Design and Prototype:** Experiment and build lots of prototypes to see what works best.

6 **Test and Reflect:** Which combinations resulted in the rocket being launched the highest? How could you improve your design?

MASS FRACTION

Rocket engineers use a calculation called **mass fraction (MF)** to measure the effectiveness of a rocket's design. Mass fraction is calculated by:

MF = mass of the propellant ÷ mass of the total rocket

The larger the MF, the smaller the payload the rocket can carry. In other words, if propellant is a larger portion of the rocket's total mass, the rocket cannot carry much payload. The trade-off, however, is that the smaller the rocket's MF, the lower its range. The most efficient rockets have an MF of approximately 0.91. The ideal rocket has 91 percent of its mass in its propellants and 6 percent in its payload. The other 3 percent is in the rocket's tanks, engines, and fins. This value allows for an effective balance between payload and range.

WORDS 2 KNOW

mass fraction (MF): a calculation used to measure the balance between payload and range, which is the effectiveness of a rocket's design.

BOUNCING BALL

Have you ever made slime? Slime is a type of polymer. A polymer is a substance with a chain-like structure, meaning there are lots of atoms connected together. A chemist figured out that you can make slime using a mixture of water, glue, borax, and cornstarch. Your job as an engineer is to take this recipe for slime and see if you can modify it to create a bouncing ball.

1 Design Goal: Create a ball that bounces—the higher, the better!

Use this basic recipe for slime as a starting point:

* In one cup, mix 4 teaspoons of white glue with 4 teaspoons of water for a 1-to-1 ratio.

* In another cup, combine 2 teaspoons of borax with 4 teaspoons of water for a 1-to-2 ratio.

* Mix until the borax is dissolved.

* Add the borax solution to the glue mixture and stir.

* The slime will begin to form immediately. Stir as much as you can, then dig in and knead it with your hands until it gets less sticky. No one makes slime without getting a little messy! Don't worry about the extra water in the cup—just pour it out. Why do you think there is extra water?

2 Question: What is the role of the glue, water, borax, and cornstarch in this recipe? How can you modify the recipe to create a bouncing ball? How can you modify the recipe further to create a ball that bounces even higher?

WORDS 2 KNOW

polymer: a substance with a chain-like structure, meaning there are lots of atoms connected together.

3 Brainstorm: Record all of your trials in your design journal. Use one variation at a time. First vary the amount of borax you use and see how the result is different, then vary the amount of glue, etc. Don't vary more than one thing at a time or you won't be able to determine what is causing a change in the behavior of the substance. Measure and record your different prototypes.

4 Select Alternatives: Select the recipe that produces the highest bouncing ball.

5 Design and Prototype: Once you have a ball that bounces, see if you can make it even more bouncy. It may take some time to figure out what works. That is okay. Keep trying!

6 Test and Reflect: Which variations in the recipe worked? Which did not? How high does your ball bounce? How would you improve your design?

STRONGER THAN STEEL

Stephanie Kwolek was a chemist who worked for a company called DuPont. She invented Kevlar, a material that is five time stronger than steel! Kevlar is a polymer. Kwolek happened upon the formula for Kevlar while trying to create a new material for tires. Kevlar is used in many things, including tires, cell phones, bulletproof vests, skis, cables, and tennis rackets.

Chapter 5
MAKING MUSIC

Do you play an instrument? Listen to music? Talk on the phone? Acoustical engineers helped design the instruments you play, the radio and MP3 player you listen to, and the phones you speak into. Engineers even designed the concert halls and auditoriums you visit to see performances. Acoustical engineers design ways to generate, record, and enhance noise and music.

WORDS 2 KNOW

acoustical engineer: an engineer who designs and builds devices related to sound and music, including hearing protection, speakers, or even music halls.

What type of instrument would you like to build? A wind instrument? A stringed instrument? A drum?

70

ESSENTIAL QUESTION

How would your life be different without music or sounds? Could you feel the **vibrations** of certain sounds? How would you adapt?

vibration: moving back and forth very quickly.

sound wave: an invisible vibration in the air that you hear as sound.

frequency: the number of sound waves that pass a specific point each second.

subjective: based on somebody's opinions or feelings rather than on facts or evidence.

WORDS 2 KNOW

Check out the guidelines at the end of the chapter to build a diddley bow, a drum, pan pipes, or an instrument of your own design!

How are noise and music similar? How are they different? Noise and music are both made up of **sound waves**. These sound waves have a range of **frequencies**. Musical sound waves tend to be ordered, while noise sound waves tend to be disordered or random.

Music is usually enjoyable to listen to, but noise is more often annoying. Music is personal and **subjective**. Some people might enjoy a certain song or musical style, while others find it hard to listen to and classify it as noise.

WHAT IS SOUND?

You can't see them, but when you listen to music, dogs barking, your friends talking, or any other noise, you are surrounded by sound waves. These sound waves have traveled through the air from the source of the sound to your ears.

Engineers use a structure called a single-degree-of-freedom-system to study sound waves. You can make your own with clay and a dowel or a mini marshmallow and strand of uncooked spaghetti.

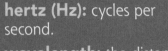
Place a lump of clay about 1 inch in diameter on top of a dowel about 1 foot long and ⅛ inch in diameter. If you hold the dowel at the bottom with one hand and pluck the lump of clay at the other end, it will move back and force at a constant rate.

Measure the time it takes for the lump of clay to move back and forth through one cycle of motion, known as the period of motion. Count the number of cycles of motion per second. This is the frequency of motion, which is measured in **hertz (Hz)**.

The time it takes for the lump of clay to return to its original position is known as the **wavelength**. If you make a graph to represent this motion, you can actually see the wave.

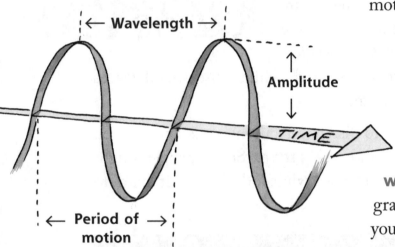

MUSIC FROM NATURE

An Aeolian wind harp is an instrument that originated in ancient Greece. Aeolian wind harps are played by the wind instead of by people! You can listen to one. Does that sound like music to you? Do you think music has to be produced by humans to be music?

Aeolian wind harps 🔍

The height of the wave, which in this case is the distance the lump of clay moves back and forth from one point to the other, is called the **amplitude**. What happens if you change the height of your model? Or the size of the clay? Will the frequency of motion change? Try it!

Decreasing the height of the dowel will increase the frequency of motion. This means the single-degree-of-freedom system will move faster. If you increase the size of the lump of clay, the frequency of motion will decrease—your system will move slower.

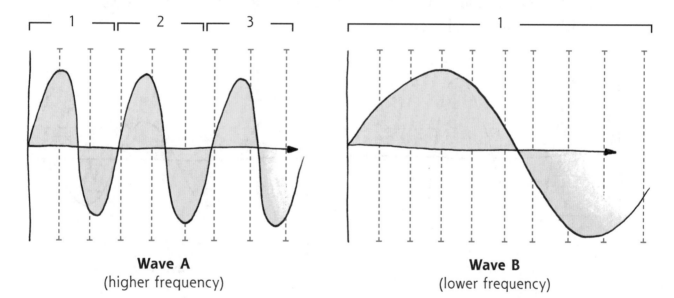

Wave A
(higher frequency)

Wave B
(lower frequency)

Playing with single-degree-of-freedom systems is fun, but what does all of this have to do with music? Consider the waves shown above. These waves could represent lumps of clay moving back and forth, but they could also represent sound waves.

We don't see sound waves, but they move through the air to reach our ears. Which kinds of waves do you think will sound low and deep like a tuba? How about high like a flute?

WORDS 2 KNOW

amplitude: the peak of a sound wave, which is associated with volume.

73

3-D ENGINEERING

A wave with a lower frequency, such as wave B (shown on the previous page), will produce a sound that is low, like a tuba. This is the sound's **pitch**. A wave with a higher frequency, such as wave A, will produce a higher sound, like a flute.

What sort of sounds do you think come from the waves shown below? They have the same wavelength and frequency, but have different amplitudes. Wave C represents a sound wave with a higher amplitude. This will produce a louder sound than wave D with a lower amplitude.

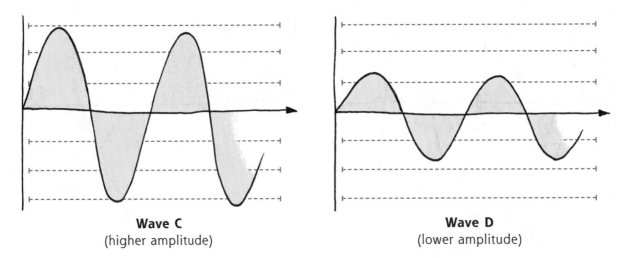

Wave C
(higher amplitude)

Wave D
(lower amplitude)

All sound, including music, is the result of vibrations. Music might be the result of the vibrations from the top of a drum or from the strings on a stringed instrument or from the vibration of air through a wind instrument. These vibrations travel as sound waves through the air to your ears and eventually to your brain, which translates the vibrations into meaningful sound.

The line between music and noise might be blurry sometimes, but in general, music is more ordered. Noise contains indistinguishable frequencies and patterns.

HOW LOUD IS LOUD?

The loudness of sound is measured in a unit called a decibel (dB). Decibels are the force of sound waves against the ear. As sounds grow louder, decibels increase. The loudness of your voice when you're talking with your friends measures approximately 65 dB. If you yell across a room to get another friend's attention, that level increases to about 95 dB.

Sound waves travel through air at a speed of about 1,115 feet per second. That translates to about 1 mile in 5 seconds!

Engineers use their understanding of sound waves when they design and build musical instruments, auditoriums, cell phones, headphones, and much more. Engineers design systems for auditoriums and music halls to enhance and direct the sound produced on stage.

They also develop ways to reduce unwanted sound or noise by designing sound barriers and hearing protection. For example, airports are often surrounded by noise barriers to reduce the impact of airplane noises on the surrounding neighborhoods.

DID YOU KNOW?

Earthquakes produce waves, too! Earthquake engineers apply the same sound principles to understand how buildings respond to earthquakes.

ESSENTIAL QUESTION

Now it's time to consider and discuss the Essential Question: How would your life be different without music or sounds? Could you feel the vibrations of certain sounds? How would you adapt?

DIDDLEY BOW

A diddley bow, also known as a slide guitar, is an instrument with a single string. To play the diddley bow, and change the frequency of the notes you are playing, you slide a glass jar or other object along the length of the string with one hand while you pluck or strike the string with the other hand.

1 **Design Goal:** Design a one-stringed diddley bow.

2 **Question:** How does the tension of the wire affect the sound of the diddley bow? How does the type and size of the wire affect the sound? How does the size and diameter of the cans or jars that you use affect the sound?

DID YOU KNOW?

Many researchers have studied the relationship between music and math. Some musicians find the Fibonacci sequence in certain pieces of music. You can listen to the music and hear an explanation here.

PS

Fibonacci sequence music 🔍

3 **Brainstorm:** Experiment with lots of different types of wire, string, cans, jars, and lengths. If you use screws to secure the wire of the diddley bow you'll easily be able to adjust the amount of tension on the wire by rotating the screw.

4 **Select Alternatives:** Test out different configurations, playing each one to see how it sounds.

5 **Design and Prototype:** All of the different design choices result in a different sound. Experiment with many different combinations to determine the best sound for your diddley bow. To build a basic diddley bow, connect a single piece of wire to two screws mounted on either end of your long board. Insert a tin can or glass jar near one end of the string to act as a bridge.

6 **Test and Reflect:** Now you are ready to play your diddley bow! Play it by plucking the wire or string with one hand, using your other hand to move the glass jar or tin can along the length of the string to adjust the vibrating length.

"I was never worried that synthesizers would replace musicians. First of all, you have to be a musician in order to make music with a synthesizer."

—Robert Moog, inventor of the Moog synthesizer

COLOSSAL INSTRUMENTS

Sometimes, great sound comes from very large packages!

The pipe organ in the Atlantic City Convention Hall in Atlantic City, New Jersey, has 33,112 pipes. The largest of the pipes, a Diaphone Profunda, is 64 feet long and made from a single tree. The organ weighs 150 tons, the size of a blue whale!

The contrabass saxophone is the largest of the woodwind instruments. A contrabass saxophone is approximately 7 feet tall! A woodwind instrument is one that produces sounds by blowing air through a cylindrical tube. Woodwinds include flutes, clarinets, saxophones, oboes, and recorders.

DRUM

IDEAS FOR SUPPLIES:
a cylindrical object such as a coffee can or oatmeal container ♦ balloon or piece of fabric or wax paper ♦ string or rubber bands ♦ items to decorate your drum

How do drums make music? When you hit the top, or head, of the drum you cause the material there to vibrate. How fast or slow the head of your drum vibrates will depend on the size of your drum, the materials you use, and how tightly the head is attached to the body of the drum.

> "I think there is something strangely musical about noise."
>
> **—Trent Reznor, songwriter, musician, and Academy Award—winning composer**

1 **Design Goal:** Design a drum to produce a high or low sound—it's your choice!

2 **Question:** Why are drums usually cylindrical? How easy is it to get the material for the top of the drum stretched tightly using a cylindrical object? How does the size of the drum affect the sound? How does the choice of material affect the sound? Should the bottom of the drum be open or closed? How will the tension in the material of the top of the drum affect the sound?

DID YOU KNOW?

A kalimba, or thumb piano, consists of a several pieces of metal, or tines, connected to a wooden box. You play a kalimba by plucking the metal tines and causing them to vibrate. kalimbas originated in Africa.

3 **Brainstorm:** Look for lots of different objects to use for your drum. Will a non-cylindrical container work? What different types of materials can you try for the top of the drum?

4 **Select Alternatives:** Be sure to select alternatives that meet your design goal of making music that you enjoy!

5 **Design and Prototype:** The best way to understand how variations in the drum design will affect the music it produces is to build lots of variations. Collect supplies and build away!

6 **Test and Reflect:** Test your drum by playing it! Does it produce the type of sound you were hoping it would? How can you change and improve the sound? What can you hit your drum with? Can you hit it in different ways to produce different sounds?

PS DIDGERI-WHO?

The didgeridoo originated in Australia more than 1,500 year ago. Didgeridoos that are flared at the end, or wider in diameter, tend to play a higher pitch than those that are not flared at the end. Can you think of some reasons why? Maybe you can design a flared instrument with an unexpected pitch!

didgeridoo 🔍

PAN PIPES

IDEAS FOR SUPPLIES:
large-diameter straws (½ inch or 12 mm-plus in diameter work better than standard drinking straws) or other cylindrical tubes such as bamboo or PVC pipe ♦ tape ♦ clay

Pan pipes or pan flutes are instruments that you use to make music by blowing across the hole at one end of a tube. Pan pipes may be open at both ends or closed at one end. It tends to be easier to play pan pipes that are closed on one end. Have you ever blown across the hole of a bottle of water? How does the sound change as the level of the water changes? These same principles apply to pan pipes.

1 Design Goal: Design a set of pan pipes that you can use to play different notes. You may choose how many different notes your pan pipes will include.

2 Question: How does the length of the straws or tubes affect the sound? Does a long tube produce a higher or lower note? How many notes do you want to include in your set of pan pipes?

3 Brainstorm: Test lots of different tube lengths. You can use clay to close off one end of the straw or tube or experiment with other materials to close off one end. Experiment with leaving both ends open.

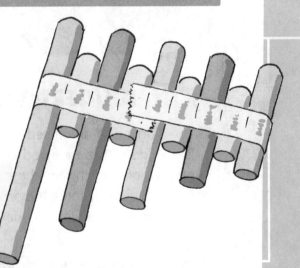

4 Select Alternatives: Which tube lengths produce the most enjoyable sounds to you? How many different lengths will you use? Do they all sound good together?

5 **Design and Prototype:** After you've tested pan pipe lengths separately, be sure to place them in sequence to see if they sound good together. When you are ready to build your "final" prototype, tape the straws or tubes together. It tends to be easier to play the pan pipes when you include some type of spacer between each separate note. A small piece of straw or tube between each note works well.

6 **Test and Reflect:** Test your pan pipes by playing them! You can extend this activity by using Audacity or a similar computer program to tune your pan pipes to specific notes.

INVENT YOUR OWN INSTRUMENT

Now that you've created some different instruments and understand more about the sound you can make, it's time to put what you've learned to work. Invent your own instrument, the more wacky and creative the better! Do you prefer a stringed instrument like the diddley bow, a wind instrument like the pan pipes, a drum, a combination, or something completely different?

Do you want it to be portable? Will you hold it? Strum it? Blow into it? What shape will it be? What materials will you use? When you're done, play your new wacky instrument! If your friends or classmates have made their own instruments, have a jam session playing them all.

Chapter 6
ELECTRIFYING DEVICES

What do lightning, your heart, an eel, and the lights in your home all have in common? All of them use electricity!

Lightning is the atmosphere's way of discharging electricity when too much **static charge** has built up. Your heartbeat is controlled by electrical impulses going through your heart. Electric eels generate electric shocks in self-defense and as a way to communicate with other eels. And the lights in your home wouldn't work without electricity.

WORDS 2 KNOW

static charge: the buildup of electrical charge on an insulated body.

? ESSENTIAL QUESTION

How would your life be different if you did not have electricity?

What electrifying devices are you interested in designing and building? Check out the guidelines for the following projects at the end of the chapter.

- A sculpture that uses dough to light up or beep!

- A dance pad.

- Your very own robot.

> "Engineering is a great profession. There is the satisfaction of watching a figment of the imagination emerge through the aid of science to a plan on paper. Then it moves to realization in stone or metal or energy."
>
> **—Herbert Hoover, 31st president of the United States**

ELECTRICAL ENGINEERING

Engineers have studied electricity since it was first discovered, and have been involved in the design of thousands of electrifying devices.

DID YOU KNOW!

Examples of biomimicry include the study of birds and bats to improve the design of aircraft and the study of moths' eyes to improve solar panels.

An engineer named Nikola Tesla invented a machine known as the Tesla coil that produces lightning, or at least what looks like lightning.

Engineers have studied how eels produce electricity to inform and improve their own designs for generating electricity. This process of looking to nature for design solutions is known as **biomimicry**.

All animals use weak electric **current** to move. But electric eels have the ability to produce a stronger charge that can paralyze or kill their prey and act as a defense mechanism.

WORDS 2 KNOW

biomimicry: the study of natural phenomenon in search of design solutions.

current: the flow of an electrical charge.

Scientists studied how electricity acts on human hearts to discover a way to develop a device to measure the health of a heart. An electrocardiogram (ECG) was designed and built by engineers. This is a test that shows the heart's electrical activity as wavy lines on a paper or screen.

The lights in your home and the electrical **circuits** in your house were also invented by engineers. They use their knowledge of electricity to create devices that are useful for us every day.

CIRCUITS

Usually we turn on light bulbs by flipping a switch. But you can make a light bulb light up with just a battery and wire. The key is to create a circuit. A circuit is a path that electricity flows along.

Using a battery, wire, and a small bulb, try to get the light bulb to glow. How many different ways can you light the light bulb? Does one way work better than others?

DID YOU KNOW?

In 1752 in his famous kite experiment, Benjamin Franklin discovered that lightning is a form of electricity.

The electricity must be able to move from one end of the battery to the light bulb, which is called the **electrical load** in a circuit. Then it must move to the other end of the battery to create a complete circuit and light the light bulb.

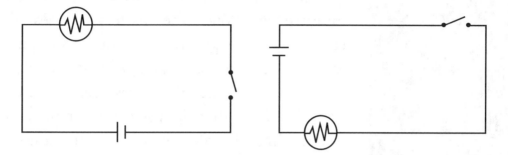

Engineers use symbols to draw the circuits that they create. Using the symbol chart below, can you find where the battery, wire, switch, and electrical load can be found on the circuit diagrams above?

Electric Circuit Symbols		
<!-- bulb symbol -->	<!-- bulb drawing -->	**Bulb**
<!-- battery symbol -->	<!-- battery drawing -->	**Battery**
<!-- wire symbol -->	<!-- wire drawing -->	**Wire**
<!-- switch symbol -->	<!-- switch drawing -->	**Switch**
<!-- connected wires symbol -->	<!-- connected wires drawing -->	**Connected Wires**
<!-- crossing wires symbol -->	<!-- crossing wires drawing -->	**Crossing Wires**

voltage: the force that moves electricity along a wire.

volts: the measure of electrical pressure. The more volts something has, the more intense or forceful it is.

amps: a measure of electrical current. Amps is the abbreviation for amperes, and it measures the number of electrons flowing per second.

WORDS 2 KNOW

Electricity is invisible, but we can see and measure its flow. The battery pushes the electricity through the circuit. This push, which is known as **voltage** and measured in **volts**, is an electrical pressure. The more pressure, the higher the voltage. Current is like the amount of water in a hose. The amount of electric current in the circuit is measured in amperes, or **amps**.

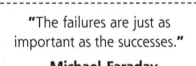

The higher the pressure, the greater the volts.

The batteries that you use in toys or radios or flashlights come in many different sizes. These batteries differ in the amount of current, or amps, they can provide, but they all have about the same amount of pressure, or voltage.

Batteries have two ends, one marked positive (+) and one marked negative (-). The current in the circuit runs from the positive end through your electric load—the light bulb, bell, motor, fan—and back through the negative end. If you

> **"The failures are just as important as the successes."**
>
> **—Michael Faraday, nineteenth-century English scientist**

flip the battery, the current will still run from positive to negative, but now your load might be connected differently. If you are using a fan as your load, the direction that the fan rotates will change.

conductor: a material through which electricity moves easily.

insulator: a material through which electric charges cannot flow.

WORDS 2 KNOW

Do you need to use wire to create a circuit? Some objects are **conductors**, meaning they transmit electricity easily. Some objects are **insulators**, meaning they will not transmit the flow of electricity. Metals such as copper and steel tend to conduct electricity, while rubber, wood, and plastic tend to be insulators. If you were creating a device to prevent electrical shocks, what would you make it out of?

DID YOU KNOW?

Computers are powered by electric circuits that turn on and off

An electrical engineer is an engineer who uses the principles of electricity to design and build devices and systems. Electrical engineers design many of the things that we use every day, from lights to computers to appliances. They also design the circuitry that brings robots to life, systems that convert energy from the sun to electricity, and microscopic circuits that may be used in the body to detect diseases.

? ESSENTIAL QUESTION

Now it's time to consider and discuss the Essential Question: How would your life be different if you did not have electricity?

DOUGHY CIRCUIT SCULPTURE

Professor AnnMarie Thomas from the University of St. Thomas developed this activity as a way for students to learn about circuits. You can read more about the project here. It's a fun activity that combines chemistry, circuits, engineering, and art. Be creative and have fun!

Squishy Circuits 🔍

1 **Design Goal:** Design a sculpture out of special conductive dough. To make the dough, mix water, flour, salt, cream of tartar, vegetable oil, and a few drops of food coloring and heat in a saucepan. Stir until it forms a ball. Let cool and knead the dough. What ingredients in this dough do you think make it conductive?

2 **Question:** Is it possible to build a circuit without wire? Can you create dough that will conduct electricity? How do the ingredients in the dough affect the circuit? What type of sculpture will you build?

3 **Brainstorm and Select Alternatives:** What type of sculpture will you build? It might be helpful to sketch many different ideas in your design journal. Plan the types and color of dough you'll need for your sculpture.

4 **Design and Prototype:** The best way to understand circuits is to build several. Mix up a batch of basic conductive dough and then start playing with circuits and building sculptures that light up. To build a basic sculpture, take two lumps of clay. Connect a wire to one end of the battery, stick the other end of this wire into one of the lumps of clay. Connect another piece of wire to the other end of the battery and stick the other end of this wire into the other lump of clay. Complete the circuit by placing each of the two wires from the light bulb into the lumps of clay—one wire into each lump. Make sure the two lumps of clay are not touching.

5 **Test and Reflect:** Create and test lots of different circuits and sculptures. You can also experiment with the dough recipe to try to make it more or less conductive.

EARLY WIRELESS

Nikola Tesla was a Serbian-American engineer who made many contributions to the development and improvement of electrical equipment in the late nineteenth and early twentieth centuries. He was one of the first people to experiment with wireless devices. He even created one of the first wireless towers, known as the Wardenclyffe Tower. Sadly, Tesla did not have enough money to make the tower successful, and it was destroyed in 1917. You can read a newspaper article about the tower from 1911.

DID YOU KNOW!

The Zeusaphone, named after the Greek god Zeus, plays music using electric shocks produced by a Tesla coil.

Tesla wireless age popular electricity 🔍

DANCE PAD

Have you ever used an arcade version of the dance pad? In this activity, you can design and build your own personal dance pad. You can find more information on building dance pads here.

dance pad mania 🔍

1 Design Goal: Design a pad that lights up or beeps when you dance on it. Not a dancer? Make an alarm pad for your room instead. Remember, you can always modify the design goal to meet your needs.

2 Question: Will your pad beep or light up? How will you protect the battery? How many zones will be included in your dance pad? How will you protect the circuit from the stomping and dancing?

3 Brainstorm: Design lots of different dance pads. It is okay to start small and add to your dance pad. Test and build as you design.

4 Select Alternatives: Select alternatives that meet your design goal!

5 Design and Prototype: Try lots of different designs. Don't get discouraged if a design fails, you've likely learned something! You'll need to include switches in your design. See if you can create a switch out of cardboard or simple materials that close the circuit when you step on it.

6 Test and Reflect: Have fun dancing. How hard do you need to dance or stomp to activate the lights or alarm? How could you improve your design?

MINI-ROBOT

IDEAS FOR SUPPLIES:

body for your robot, such as the top of a toothbrush, a wine cork, or an eraser ♦ watch battery ♦ pager motor or other type of small, vibrating motor ♦ hot glue

There are lots of options for building robots. Start with a simple mini-robot that moves around and see where you can go from there! You can see toothbrush robots being made here.

how to make a bristlebot 🔍

1 **Design Goal:** Design a robot that moves by vibrating.

2 **Question:** What will your robot do? How does the size and weight of the robot affect the motion? What type of motor will you use?

3 **Brainstorm:** Look for lots of different objects to use for your robot. Try different objects for the body and motor and decorate them.

4 **Select Alternatives:** Select alternatives that meet your design goal.

5 **Design and Prototype:** Test lots of different types of robots. To make a simple vibrating robot, attach the motor to the top of the robot body you've chosen. Connect each of the wires from the motor to one side of the battery. Turn on the motor and watch your robot move.

6 **Test and Reflect:** How well does your robot move? Can you modify it to make it move more or less? What did you learn? How could you improve your design?

Chapter 7

ENERGY CONVERTERS

We use energy in every aspect of our lives. Energy is needed to heat our homes, run our lights and appliances, and fuel our cars and our bodies. Engineers design and build the devices that we need to convert, store, and use energy, from power plants to batteries to televisions to computers.

How can we convert one form of energy to another? You can find guidelines to some ideas at the end of the chapter. These include building a solar cooker, designing a device that uses the wind to lift messages, and building a water-powered hammer!

DID YOU KNOW?

The word energy is based on the Greek word *energeia*, which means "activity."

What types of energy do you use every day to keep your body moving, to heat or cool your house, and to get from place to place?

There are two main types of energy—**kinetic energy** and **potential energy**. Kinetic energy is the energy associated with motion. Potential energy is stored energy.

A carrot contains potential energy that you eat and convert to kinetic energy that you use to run and play. Energy comes in many forms, including **solar**, **geothermal**, **mechanical**, **electrical**, **chemical**, and **nuclear**. Where do you think the energy in that carrot comes from?

kinetic energy: energy associated with motion.

potential energy: stored energy.

solar energy: energy from the sun.

geothermal energy: energy from below the surface of the earth. It can heat and cool by using differences in temperature between a structure and the earth.

mechanical energy: energy related to motion and height.

electrical energy: energy related to electricity.

chemical energy: energy from a chemical reaction.

nuclear energy: energy produced by a nuclear reaction, typically the splitting of an atom.

non-renewable resource: a resource that gets used up and may not be readily replaced, such as oil.

renewable resource: a resource that cannot be used up, such as solar energy.

WORDS 2 KNOW

Energy comes from many sources. Most of the energy we use comes from **non-renewable resources**, but increasingly we are turning to **renewable resources** for energy.

3-D ENGINEERING

fossil fuels: coal, oil, and natural gas. These energy sources come from the fossils of plants and animals that lived millions of years ago. It takes hundreds of millions years for fossil fuels to form, so they are non-renewable resources.

thermal mass: a material that stores heat and releases it slowly.

WORDS 2 KNOW

Non-renewable resources, such as coal and oil, are not easily replenished. These non-renewable energy sources are also known as **fossil fuels** since they were created by applying pressure and heat to fossils through millions of years. Renewable resources are those that can be replenished, such as solar, wind, and geothermal.

SOLAR

The sun is the key to most of our energy. The energy from the sun can be used directly as solar lighting and heating. The sun also provides energy for the plants that animals eat. Even wind is the result of the uneven heating of the earth by the sun. Everything comes back to the sun, our main source of energy.

One of the easiest ways to use energy from the sun is to convert it to heat.

People have been passively heating their homes with solar energy for many years. When you sit inside by the window on a sunny day and feel warm, you are experiencing heat from passive solar energy. Architects often design homes, especially in colder climates, to maximize the amount of heat gained passively from the sun. Passive solar heating strategies include south-facing windows and **thermal masses**.

94

A thermal mass is a structure made out of a material that is able to store heat, such as concrete or brick. The thermal mass stores the heat for future use. Passive solar energy is energy gained through non-mechanical means.

Solar hot water heaters also use the energy from the sun to heat water. Have you ever left a water bottle out in the sun at the beach? What happens to it? Tanks holding lots of water can be heated the same way.

What materials do you think work well as thermal masses? Test different materials by setting them out in the sun and then measuring the temperatures of the materials at different times. Which materials store the most heat? Which materials retain the heat the longest?

Energy from the sun can also be converted to electricity. The most common way to convert solar energy to electricity is through **photovoltaics**.

WORDS 2 KNOW

photovoltaic: a device that produces electricity when exposed to sunlight.

kilowatt-hour (kWh): a unit of work or energy equal to the amount produced by one kilowatt in one hour.

MEASURING ENERGY

Energy can be measured. Common units for energy include the joule and the kilowatt-hour. Your monthly electric bill is probably based on the amount of **kilowatt-hours (kWh)** of electricity your family uses during the month, or the total quantity of electrical energy that your family uses to run lights and appliances. Look at your electric bill from last month. How many kilowatt-hours did your family use?

Photovoltaics use **semiconductors** to convert solar energy to electricity. When certain types of semiconductors are exposed to sunlight, an electric current can be developed. Have you ever seen solar panels on the roof of a house? These are panels of photovoltaics. Engineers work to create new, more efficient types of semiconductor materials that might be used as photovoltaics.

WIND AND WATER

Engineers design systems to convert the energy found all around us to usable sources of energy. One way to convert energy is with a turbine. For example, wind and water turbines convert the kinetic energy of the motion of wind and water to the potential energy of electricity that can be used to light our homes, power our televisions, and run our computers and appliances.

Power plants also convert fossil fuels such as coal and oil to electricity using turbines. So how do turbines work? Let's take a closer look.

First, let's consider windmills. Some people use the words "windmill" and "wind turbine" interchangeably, but they mean different things. Windmills have been around for many, many years. They are used to convert the energy in the wind to a rotational or mechanical form of energy. As the windmill turns, it rotates a shaft, or long circular rod, that can be used to do work.

Think about a windmill lifting a bucket of water. The windmill turns and makes a shaft move upward to lift the bucket. This is a form of mechanical energy. In the past, windmills were mainly used to pump water and grind grain through mechanical means.

A windmill converts the energy in the wind to mechanical energy. A wind turbine is typically used to generate electrical energy, not mechanical energy.

Turbine spins shaft

Spinning coil of wire

MAGNET (N)

MAGNET (S)

Direction of current

The wind causes the blades of the wind turbine to rotate. These blades are connected to a shaft that spins. Wire is connected to the shaft, and magnets are placed on both sides of the shaft. The spinning shaft and the magnets together convert the spinning motion into electrical energy.

How much energy can a wind turbine convert to electricity? It depends a lot on the speed of the wind and the radius of the turbine.

One wind turbine with blades that are 164 feet long is able to convert enough energy from the wind to provide electricity for about 150 homes. A typical family in New England uses about 8,500 kWh of electricity each year.

more wind at high speeds = more electricity
longer blades = more electricity

Engineers look for locations with steady, high-**velocity** winds for their wind turbines. The faster the shaft of the wind turbine spins, the more energy is converted to electricity.

Gears are often used to increase the speed of the shaft. What do you remember about gears from Chapter 2? How might engineers position gears to increase the amount of electricity produced by a turbine?

Water turbines and **hydroelectric** plants work like wind turbines. Instead of using wind, they use the motion of water to spin the shafts. Power plants that use fossil fuels to produce electricity use steam to turn the turbines. In these power plants, fossils fuels are burned to boil water and create steam, which rotates the turbines.

GEOTHERMAL

Geothermal systems can be used to both heat and cool buildings. It works by using the differences in temperature between the building and the earth.

DID YOU KNOW?

Around 1832, an English scientist named Michael Faraday discovered that combining magnets, wire, and rotation resulted in electricity.

In the winter, it is warmer underground than aboveground. Water is pumped through pipes installed in the earth, where it is heated by the earth's natural heat. In the summer, the opposite is true. Underground is cooler than aboveground. Water is pumped through the pipes to be cooled.

This constant cycle of heating and cooling requires very little energy—just enough to run the pump.

WORLD ENERGY CONSUMPTION

The world continues to consume large amounts of energy, most of which is still supplied by fossil fuels. To date, less than 20 percent of the world's energy comes from renewable sources. Solar, wind, and geothermal energy together provide less than 1 percent of the world's energy. While the United States is one of the top producers of geothermal, wind, and solar energy in the world, it is also one of the biggest consumers of energy. How can we encourage people to turn to renewable energy sources? How can we reduce energy consumption? What steps can you and your family take to reduce energy consumption? Look at this chart showing the world's energy consumption. Which renewable energy do you hope the United States will focus on in the future?

world energy consumption chart 🔍

99

THE PROS AND CONS OF ENERGY SOURCES

Humans consume lots of energy for a wide range of activities. While renewable energy might seem like the answer, there are pros and cons to all energy sources.

Below is a list of energy source pros and cons. Can you think of other pros and cons? What energy sources do you recommend? How could engineers improve on the negative aspects of each source?

Source	Pros	Cons
Coal	Cheap and reliable.	Non-renewable. Contributes to climate change.
Natural Gas	Cleaner than coal.	Non-renewable. Poses environmental risks.
Oil	Easy to extract, handle, and store.	Non-renewable. Contributes to climate change. Poses environmental risks.
Nuclear	Produces lots of energy. Produces no air pollution.	Non-renewable. Can be very destructive to the environment. Poses human risk.
Solar	Produces no noise or air pollution.	High cost. Takes up land. Can't use everywhere.
Wind	Uses less land than solar panels. Produces no air pollution.	Requires wind. Produces noise and impacts wildlife. Has a visual impact.
Water	Produces no air pollution. Does not use any fuel.	Expensive. Large environmental impact from dams.
Geothermal	Produces no air pollution. Does not use any fuel.	Poses environmental risks. Can't use everywhere.

Engineers are continually trying to improve renewable energy systems. A big area of research is energy storage, in terms of how we efficiently store the energy we convert to electricity from solar, wind, and other sources. Engineers also work on reducing the impact and waste of other energy sources to improve the environment.

? ESSENTIAL QUESTION

Now it's time to consider and discuss the Essential Question: What types of energy do you use every day to keep your body moving, to heat or cool your house, and to get from place to place?

SOLAR COOKER

A solar cooker converts sunlight to heat energy. Think about heat absorption and experiment with different materials. While it takes longer to cook using solar cookers, the energy from the sun is free and the air is not polluted by cooking with it.

DID YOU KNOW?

The temperature inside a well-designed solar cooker can reach as high as 300 degrees Fahrenheit.

1 **Design Goal:** Design a device to cook something, such as a s'more or cheese sandwich.

2 **Question:** What size box will allow you to collect more heat? Is it better to use a deep or shallow box? Should the box be closed or open? Could you insulate the box? Does it help to insulate the box?

3 **Brainstorm:** Look for different types of boxes for your solar cooker. Try painting the box, insulating it, covering it, and adding reflective pieces.

4 **Select Alternatives:** You'll need to build and test solar cookers before you can select the best one. Jump in and start building!

5 **Design and Prototype, Test and Reflect:** Put a thermometer in your solar cooker to check the temperature. Which design reaches the highest temperature? How could you improve your design? Is a solar cooker a viable alternative to your standard oven? Why or why not?

101

WIND-POWERED MESSAGE LIFTER

IDEAS FOR SUPPLIES:

wooden dowels or bamboo skewers ◆ paper plates ◆ cardboard ◆ Styrofoam ball ◆ tape or glue ◆ milk carton or 2-liter soda bottle ◆ paperclip or hook

Windmills are used to convert energy from the wind to mechanical energy, often to pump or lift water. See if you can use these same principles to lift a written message.

1 Design Goal: Design a device that converts the wind to rotational motion to lift a message from the ground to a desired height. You can decide where you want to use your wind-powered message lifter—on a porch, balcony, treehouse, tree, or table.

2 Question: How many blades will you use? How large will the blades be? What shape will the blades be? Will they be angled? How will you connect your message to the string? How fast do you want to be able to lift your message? Do some planning in your design journal.

3 Brainstorm and Select Alternatives: Experiment with lots of different blade designs and maybe do some research on windmills and wind turbines. Do the blades of windmills and wind turbines look the same or different? Why are they made this way?

4 Design and Prototype: The basic idea for the wind device is to use the milk carton as a tower or support with a skewer or dowel running through it to act as the shaft. Attach a string to one end of the dowel or skewer for the messages and use the other end for the blades. A Styrofoam ball works well for attaching the blades to the shaft, but other things could work too, such as clay or cardboard and tape. The design of the blades of your wind-powered message lifter will determine how heavy a message can be and how fast it can be lifted. Experiment with lots of different designs.

5 Test and Reflect: How does your message lifter work? How could you improve the design? Could you lift something heavier with your wind-powered lifting machine? Give it a try!

WINDY FARMS

Out on the ocean, wind speeds tend to be greater and more consistent, and there are fewer obstructions. This makes the ocean a terrific place for wind farms. Engineers are even designing and building floating wind turbines. One of the downsides to ocean wind farms is that long wires must be used to carry the electricity from the ocean to where it is needed on land. Can you think of different ways of getting that renewable energy to shore where people can use it?

WATER-POWERED HAMMER

A common use of water wheels was to crush grain. A hammer-type device was lifted and dropped with a cam that was rotated using the motion of the water. A cam is an unsymmetrical piece that is attached to the rotating shaft that turns a rotating motion into a linear motion.

1 **Design Goal:** Design a water-powered hammer. How do you want to use your hammer? Maybe you want to crush a cracker or stamp a design!

2 **Question:** How many cups should you use? How heavy is the hammer? How will you make the cam? What will you crush or stamp? What's your water source?

3 **Brainstorm:** Come up with lots of design ideas for your waterwheel, hammer, and the support.

4 **Design and Prototype:** Use cups or spoons for the paddles of your waterwheel. Attach them to a plastic plate or disc of Styrofoam. Use a dowel or skewer for the shaft, with the waterwheel attached at one end and a cam at the other end. The 2-liter soda bottle can support your waterwheel.

5 **Test and Reflect:** Test your waterwheel by pouring into the paddles. Do the cam and hammer work? Does the cam lift the hammer as high as you'd hoped? How could you modify your design?

Chapter 8

DESIGN AND BUILD PROTOTYPES

Now that you've learned about some of the different principles that go into engineering design, you're ready to design and build your own prototypes or improve the prototypes you've already built. This is a great way to better understand how engineering principles affect all the products and processes you use every day.

Remember, don't be afraid to tackle difficult problems. And don't get discouraged when your prototypes don't work perfectly the first time!

? ESSENTIAL QUESTION

How can you apply engineering design principles to design and build engineering solutions for yourself, your family, your home, and your school?

When making your prototypes, remember to use the engineering design process that was outlined at the beginning of the book.

1 Identify the design goal

2 Ask questions to clarify the goal

3 Redefine the goal based on the answers

4 Brainstorm ways to meet the goal

5 Select alternatives

6 Design and prototype

7 Test your prototype

8 Redesign

HUMAN-CENTERED DESIGN

One of the best ways to identify problems or needs is to interact with users and follow a **human-centered** approach. This means carefully considering the needs and desires of the user during your design process.

Human-centered designers spend long hours interviewing and observing users to gather information. They ask users to test their prototypes as they design them, and observe carefully how they interact with the prototypes. Then they make adjustments as needed.

> "Design thinking is a human-centered approach to innovation that draws from the designer's toolkit to integrate the needs of people, the possibilities of technology, and the requirements for business success."
>
> **—Tim Brown, CEO of IDEO**

Designers who don't use a human-centered approach might build a device and then try to convince people they need it. Focusing on the needs and desires of users throughout the design process can produce more useful products.

WORDS 2 KNOW

human-centered: a design approach in which the needs of the human user are a top priority.

innovative: having new ideas about how something can be done.

WORDS 2 KNOW

REDESIGN OF THE SHOPPING CART

One example of human-centered design is the redesign of the shopping cart by engineers at IDEO. This award-winning company specializes in **innovative** solutions for a wide range of problems. IDEO was founded in 1991 by David Kelley, and the company currently has offices and clients around the world.

The shopping cart redesign was a challenge taken on by a diverse team of designers that included several engineers. In four days, the team completely redesigned the shopping cart. The goal was to improve the cart's mobility and the safety of children riding in the cart, as well as to reduce maintenance costs.

Rather than start by just looking at an existing cart, the designers spent the first day of the challenge observing shoppers to understand their behavior.

IDEO designers observed that shoppers often left their carts to grab different items and often spent much of their time waiting in line to checkout. They also observed that existing carts were not only bulky, they had wheels that didn't always function. The single basket for groceries made it difficult for users to organize their merchandise.

DAVID KELLEY

David Kelley pioneered human-centered design. Kelley is the founder of IDEO, the award-winning design firm that created the new, human-centered shopping cart. He is also a professor of engineering at Stanford University, where he heads the design school, which is focused on design thinking. Kelley, along with his brother, Tom, has spent most of his life designing, building, and innovating.

Based on what they observed, IDEO's designers and engineers established a design goal. Then they built prototypes, from very simple to more elaborate, and continued to evaluate and adapt their design. The redesigned shopping cart is sleek and relies on the use of several removable baskets rather than a single large container. It also has a scanner attached so that users can scan their purchases as they shop. Why do you think this is a useful feature?

DID YOU KNOW!

IDEO's redesign of the shopping cart is the focus of an ABC *Nightline* episode called "Deep Dive."

Deep Dive ABC Nightline 🔍

COMPUTER TOOLS FOR DESIGN

Engineers and designers often use computers to draw and build prototypes. Different computer programs are helpful in different ways, depending on the goals of the engineer.

LIVING IN SHAPES

Frank Gehry is a famous architect who designed the Guggenheim Museum Bilbao, among many other buildings. One of his first design projects was a line of furniture made out of cardboard called Easy Edges. He soon began designing buildings, and now uses computer software extensively in his designs. Gehry even started his own company that develops design software.

Computer-aided design (CAD) programs such as SketchUp, Make, SolidWorks, and AutoCAD are used by engineers to create two-dimensional (2-D) and three-dimensional (3-D) images of their designs. There are advantages of using CAD software.

computer-aided design (CAD): software used to create two-dimensional and three-dimensional drawings.

analyze: to study and examine.

WORDS 2 KNOW

- You can share your drawings electronically.

- You can make changes quickly, and objects you draw can be easily rotated to show different views.

- Many CAD programs will also allow you to **analyze** your device to better understand how it will work and behave.

- In most cases, you can save your CAD designs in a format that can be used by a machine to manufacture your device.

To try using a CAD program, download the free version of SketchUp at sketchup.com. You can watch video tutorials that will help you learn the program.

3-D ENGINEERING

WORDS 2 KNOW

Computer-aided manufacturing (CAM) involves using computers to manufacture or machine prototypes and parts. Objects that can be created using CAM range from small parts for your computer or iPhone to toys and machines to parts of buildings and airplanes. There are several machines that used CAM:

- **laser-cutters** cut 2-D objects from wood and plastic using a laser

- **milling machines** use a rotating cutter to remove material

- **lathes** cut away material from an object as it spins

- **3-D printers** print parts and objects directly using a range of different materials

Through designing and building, you can improve the world around you and learn a great deal about how things work. You can design products and processes to improve your daily life or the lives of others in need using the engineering design process.

? ESSENTIAL QUESTION

Now it's time to consider and discuss the Essential Question: How can you apply engineering design principles to design and build engineering solutions for yourself, your family, your home, and your school?

CLEANING UP OUR WORLD

Pollution comes in the form of litter, smog, chemicals in the air, oil in our water, and poisons in the ground. Engineers work to design new devices to clean up the environment, such as scrubbers that remove pollutants from furnaces in large plants or sorbents to recover liquids, including oil from oil spills.

1 Design Goal: Design a way to reduce or clean up a certain type of pollution.

DID YOU KNOW!

A new device called Clarity allows users to determine the level of air pollution near them using a small, wearable device.

2 Question: Do some research into different types of pollution and existing approaches to reducing pollution or cleaning up polluted sites. What types of pollution exist in and around your home and neighborhood? How are they being addressed? Maybe you can observe people in your city and try to figure out why some people litter or why others don't recycle.

3 Design and Prototype: Your design may end up being a device, such as some type of filter or sorbent, but it could also be a process. Maybe you can come up with a way to encourage people to recycle or a process for composting waste in your school cafeteria.

4 Test and Reflect: Test your device to make sure it works as you planned. And reflect on the process: What worked and what didn't work? How could your device or process be improved?

IMPROVING HEALTH AND MOBILITY

Engineers often work with doctors and medical professionals to design devices to improve health, cure diseases, and help people overcome disabilities. For example, engineers design prosthetic limbs to replace missing knees, arms, legs, and other body parts. Engineers also design and build machines to detect diseases and devices to inject medicines.

1 **Design Goal:** Design a device to improve health, cure a disease, or help people overcome a disability.

2 **Question:** Be sure to observe and talk to users. What are their needs and problems? Maybe you want to tackle obesity—how can you get people to be more active? Can you design a new game that encourages people to move around? Maybe you can think of ways for people to track the food that they eat. What types of disabilities do people have? How can they be overcome? What types of devices or processes might help?

3 **Brainstorm:** While you may not be able to design a new protein or cure cancer, you can brainstorm ways to tackle big issues. You might be surprised by what you can come up with!

WORDS 2 KNOW

prosthetic: an artificial body part.

magnetic resonance imaging (MRI) machine: a machine used to see inside the body.

sedate: to give a person or an animal drugs that make them relax or sleep.

	SUN	MON	TUE	WED	THU	FRI	SAT
SITUPS							
WALK							
SPORTS							
BIKE							
SWIM							
PUSHUPS							
SKATE							
JUMPING JACKS							
DANCE							
JUMP ROPE							
HULA HOOP							

4 **Design and Prototype:** Design and build some simple prototypes. Maybe you can design a cane for someone in your family or at a nearby nursing home or think of a better way for kids to take medicine, since pills are tough to swallow. Consider ideas for fun new games to get people moving. Write down your ideas, test them on your friends, build any necessary devices that you need, and have fun!

5 **Test and Reflect:** Were your devices and processes successful? Be sure to have users test your prototypes and give you feedback. How could they be improved?

MRI MACHINE

Another example of human-centered design is the redesign of the **magnetic resonance imaging (MRI) machine**. An MRI is a machine used to see inside the body.

Doug Dietz, a designer at General Electric, decided to redesign the MRI machine after observing children having an MRI. These machines work great from a technical standpoint, but they look like a deep tunnel. Children were terrified of going into the machine, and often needed to be **sedated** before a scan.

Doug took a course in human-centered design at Stanford's design school, which is focused on design thinking. Then, he redesigned the MRI experience for children by transforming his MRI machines into pirate ships and spaceships. Does that sound less scary than big tubes? Now, children rarely need to be sedated when using one of these newly designed MRIs.

DEVICES FOR SOCIAL GOOD

Access to clean water, plumbing, and energy continue to be major problems around the world. In many regions, electricity is not available and people must walk for miles to collect water that must then be filtered or boiled to make it safe to drink. In some parts of the world, indoor plumbing and bathrooms are rare.

1 **Design Goal:** Design a device or process for a social good that solves problems of low-cost housing, the need to filter water, the need for an inexpensive way to produce light, or something else. There are plenty of social needs to choose from!

2 **Question:** What types of needs and problems exist? How are these needs currently being tackled? What improvements or innovations can be made? What types of materials are available to build inexpensive, efficient devices?

3 **Design and Prototype:**
Design and build lots of prototypes. Maybe you start with a design that someone else has used but then change it somehow. Many people have built filters to clean water, but maybe your designs and experiments will take you in a new direction. Successful designs are often the result of accidental experiments.

4 Test and Reflect: Did your devices or prototypes meet the needs of the people you were trying to help? How could the users be more involved in the process? How could your prototype be improved?

> "There's nothing I believe in more strongly than getting young people interested in science and engineering for a better tomorrow for all humankind."
>
> **—Bill Nye, American science educator**

DESIGNS FOR THE GREATER GOOD

The urge to improve lives has always been good motivation for engineers. Here are a few designs that are making a difference.

❏ Engineers at IDEO recently developed the Aquaduct, a bicycle that may be used to transport, filter, and store water.

❏ In 2011, the Gates Foundation established the Reinvent the Toilet Challenge. Through this challenge, individuals, groups, and companies were awarded grants to develop ways to safely and sustainably manage human waste.

> reinvent the toilet challenge 🔎

❏ A company called LuminAID designed and built an inflatable light source that is very portable and uses stored solar energy to produce light. These light sources are invaluable in areas where electricity is not available, such as developing countries or in areas hit by natural disasters.

> LuminAID 🔎

❏ The $300 House project was started by a business professor at Dartmouth College and a consultant. The pair wrote an article challenging the world to design a house that could be built for $300. Many, many people took on the challenge, and engineers and architects around the world continue to try to design and develop affordable housing for the poor.

> $300 House 🔎

3-D printer: a machine that prints 3-D objects using a range of different materials.

acoustical engineer: an engineer who designs and builds devices related to sound and music, including hearing protection, speakers, or even music halls.

aerodynamic: having a shape that reduces the amount of drag when moving through the air or water, enabling a shape to move quickly through the air or water.

amplitude: the peak of a sound wave, which is associated with volume.

amps: a measure of electrical current. Amps is the abbreviation for amperes, and it measures the number of electrons flowing per second.

analog: presenting data as a measurable physical quality, not as numbers.

analyze: to study and examine.

applied load: a load that is being used.

atom: a small particle of matter. Atoms combine to form molecules.

axis: the center, around which something rotates.

axis: the center, around which something rotates.

beam: a structural element that resists bending under the weight of a load.

biomimicry: the study of natural phenomenon in search of design solutions.

brainstorm: to think creatively and without judgment, often in a group of people.

buckle: to collapse in the middle.

buoyancy: the upward force from a fluid that helps an object float.

carbon dioxide: a gas in the air made of carbon and oxygen atoms.

center of gravity: the point on any object where all the weight is centered.

chemical energy: energy from a chemical reaction.

chemical engineer: a scientist who uses chemistry to solve problems and design new products and processes.

chemical reaction: the combination of two or more substances that results in a completely new chemical substance.

chemistry: the study of how matter changes.

circuit: a path that lets electricity flow when closed in a loop.

circumference: the distance around the edge of a circle.

collapse: to fall in or down suddenly.

compression: a pushing force that squeezes or presses a material inward.

computer-aided design (CAD): software used to create two-dimensional and three-dimensional drawings.

computer-aided manufacturing (CAM): the use of computers to manufacture a part or prototype.

conductor: a material through which electricity moves easily.

crush: to break apart.

current: the flow of an electrical charge.

cylindrical: round.

deflection: changing shape under the weight of a load.

density: the amount of matter in a given space, or mass divided by volume.

displacement: the amount a beam moves due to an applied load.

dissolve: to mix with a liquid and become part of the liquid.

drag: a force that acts to slow down an object in air.

drift: to move freely on the water.

electrical energy: energy related to electricity.

electrical load: the part of a circuit that consumes the electric power. Examples include light bulbs and fans.

endothermic: a reaction that absorbs heat.

energy: the ability to do work or cause change.

engineer: someone who uses science, math, and creativity to design products or processes to meet human needs or solve problems.

exothermic: a reaction that produces heat.

flink: a combination of floating and sinking. When something flinks it hovers in the water.

fluid: a substance such as a gas or a liquid that flows freely and has no fixed shape.

force: a push or a pull.

fossil fuels: coal, oil, and natural gas. These energy sources come from the fossils of plants and animals that lived millions of years ago. It takes hundreds of millions years for fossil fuels to form, so they are non-renewable resources.

frequency: the number of sound waves that pass a specific point each second.

friction: a force that resists motion.

gear: a rotating part with teeth.

gear ratio: the rate the first gear rotates divided by the rate the last gear rotates.

gear train: a system of gears that transmits motion from one gear to the next.

geothermal energy: energy from below the surface of the earth. It can heat and cool by using differences in temperature between a structure and the earth.

glucose: a type of sugar a plant makes for food.

gusset plate: a sheet of material that is applied to the outside of multiple members to connect them.

hertz (Hz): cycles per second.

hover: to float without moving.

hull: the body of a ship.

human-centered: a design approach in which the needs of the human user or human are a top priority.

hydroelectric: converting energy from moving water to electricity.

iceberg: a large piece of floating ice.

innovative: having new ideas about how something can be done.

instability: not stable.

insulator: a material through which electric charges cannot flow.

kilowatt-hour (kWh): a unit of work or energy equal to the amount produced by one kilowatt in one hour.

kinetic energy: energy associated with motion.

laser-cutter: a machine that cuts 2-D forms using a laser.

lathe: a machine that removes material from an object as it spins to create a part.

lift: an upward force due to the motion of an object through the air.

load: the weight of something.

magnetic resonance imaging (MRI) machine: a machine used to see inside the body.

mass fraction (MF): a calculation used to measure the balance between payload and range, which is the effectiveness of a rocket's design.

mass: the amount of matter in an object.

matter: anything that has weight and takes up space.

mechanical energy: energy related to motion and height.

member: a component of a structure such as a truss member or beam.

milling machine: a machine that uses a rotating cutter to remove material to create an object.

mixture: the physical combination of two or more substances, but without any chemical reaction.

molecule: a group of atoms bound together. Molecules combine to form matter.

moment of inertia: the measure of an object's resistance to bending. It is a geometrical property that relates to the distribution of mass in a shape.

non-renewable resource: a resource that gets used up and may not be readily replaced, such as oil.

nuclear energy: energy produced by a nuclear reaction, typically the splitting of an atom.

optical illusion: a trick of the eyes that makes people see something differently than it really is.

orientation: the position of a beam relative to the applied load.

phase: the physical form that matter takes, such as a solid, liquid, or gas. Also called states of matter.

photosynthesis: the process through which plants change carbon dioxide, water, and light into glucose and oxygen.

photovoltaic: a device that produces electricity when exposed to sunlight.

pitch: how high or low a sound is, depending on its frequency.

polymer: a substance with a chain-like structure, meaning there are lots of atoms connected together.

potential energy: stored energy.

power: energy used through time.

process: an activity that takes several steps to complete.

product: an item, such as a book or clothing, that is made and sold to people.

prosthetic: an artificial body part.

prototype: a working model or mock-up that allows engineers to test their solution.

radius: the distance from the center of a circle to the outside edge of the circle.

redefine: to define differently or think about a problem in a new way.

renewable resource: a resource that cannot be used up, such as solar energy.

resistance: a force that slows down another force.

revolution: one complete turn made by something moving in a circle around a fixed point.

rotational motion: the spinning motion around a central axis.

saturated: a solvent that is no longer able to dissolve any more solute.

scientific principle: a rule that explains a natural action that can be tested.

sedate: to give a person or an animal drugs that make them relax or sleep.

semiconductor: a material that conducts some electricity.

simultaneously: at the same time.

solar energy: energy from the sun.

solute: the dissolved substance in a solution.

solution: the chemical combination of two or more substances.

solvent: the substance into which a solute dissolves (often water).

sound wave: an invisible vibration in the air that you hear as sound.

span: the distance between supports.

stability: the ability of an object to maintain a certain position without collapsing.

static charge: the buildup of electrical charge on an insulated body.

stiffness: the ability of an object to resist deflecting or moving when a load is applied.

strength: the ability of an object to support a load before breaking.

structural: relating to the way something is built.

structure: something that is built, such as a building, bridge, tunnel, tower, or dam.

subjective: based on somebody's opinions or feelings rather than on facts or evidence.

substance: matter with specific properties.

symmetrical: the same on all sides.

technology: tools, methods, and systems used to solve a problem or do work.

tension: a pulling force that pulls or stretches an object.

thaumatrope: a popular nineteenth-century spinning toy.

thermal mass: a material that stores heat and releases it slowly.

transmit: to send or pass something from one place or person to another.

GLOSSARY

truss: a structure composed of slender members connected at the ends such that the members form strong triangles.

turbine: a machine with blades turned by the force of water, air, or steam.

velocity: the speed an object moves in a particular directions.

vibration: moving back and forth very quickly.

voltage: the force that moves electricity along a wire.

volts: the measure of electrical pressure. The more volts something has, the more intense or forceful it is.

volume: the amount of space an object takes up.

wavelength: the distance from the high point of one wave to the high point of the next wave.

weight: a measure of the force of gravity on an object.

windmill: a device that converts the energy of the wind to mechanical energy.

METRIC CONVERSIONS

Use this chart to find the metric equivalents to the English measurements in this book. If you need to know a half measurement, divide by two. If you need to know twice the measurement, multiply by two. How do you find a quarter measurement? How do you find three times the measurement?

English	Metric
1 inch	2.5 centimeters
1 foot	30.5 centimeters
1 yard	0.9 meter
1 mile	1.6 kilometers
1 pound	0.5 kilogram
1 teaspoon	5 milliliters
1 tablespoon	15 milliliters
1 cup	237 milliliters

BOOKS

Gizmos & Gadgets: Creating Science Contraptions that Work (& Knowing Why).
Jill Frankel Hauser. Williamson Publishing, 1999.

Gourmet Lab: The Scientific Principles Behind Your Favorite Foods. Sarah Reeves Young.
National Science Teachers Association Press, 2011.

Make Your Own Musical Instruments. Anna-Marie D'Cruz. PowerKids Press, 2009.

Making Things Move: DIY Mechanisms for Inventors, Hobbyists, and Artists.
Dustyn Roberts. McGraw-Hill Education, 2010.

Music and Mathematics: From Pythagoras to Fractals. Edited by John Fauvel,
Raymond Flood, and Robin Wilson. Oxford University Press, 2006.

Spinning. Sara E. Hoffmann. Lerner Classroom, 2012.

The Art of Construction: Projects and Principles for Beginning Engineers & Architects.
Mario Salvadori. Chicago Review Press, 2000.

The Art of Tinkering. Karen Wilkinson and Mike Petrich. Weldon Owen, 2014.

The New Way Things Work. David Macaulay. HMH, 1998.

WEBSITES

About Chemistry: chemistry.about.com/od/letsmakeslime/tp/slimerecipes.htm

Chem4Kids: chem4kids.com

Engineering Encounters - Bridge Design Contest: bridgecontest.org

How Stuff Works - Gear Ratios:
science.howstuffworks.com/transport/engines-equipment/gear-ratio.htm

How Things Fly: howthingsfly.si.edu/gravity-air/buoyancy

PBS Building Big: pbs.org/wgbh/buildingbig/bridge

PBS Nova: pbs.org/wgbh/nova/physics/galileo-experiments.html

PBS Parents: pbs.org/parents/crafts-for-kids/super-bouncy-balls

PhET Interactive Simulations: phet.colorado.edu/en/simulation/density

Squishy Circuits: courseweb.stthomas.edu/apthomas/SquishyCircuits

TED-ED: Archimedes' Principle:
ed.ted.com/lessons/mark-salata-how-taking-a-bath-led-to-archimedes-principle

ARTICLES

Haugh, Thomas (2002). *Snow Globe Science.* The Science Teacher. 69(3): pp. 36-39.

QR CODE INDEX

ESSENTIAL QUESTIONS

Introduction: What is engineering and how does it impact your life?

Chapter 1: How does an engineer design a structure to support a load?

Chapter 2: What factors affect the way something spins?

Chapter 3: How does buoyancy help you float? How does lift help keep an airplane aloft?

Chapter 4: What would life be like without the phase changes of matter? If water never turned to snow or ice or steam? If milk never turned to ice cream?!

Chapter 5: How would your life be different without music or sounds? Could you feel the vibrations of certain sounds? How would you adapt?

Chapter 6: How would your life be different if you did not have electricity?

Chapter 7: What types of energy do you use every day to keep your body moving, to heat or cool your house, and to get from place to place?

Chapter 8: How can you apply engineering design principles to design and build engineering solutions for yourself, your family, your home, and your school?

INDEX